REPUBLICANS ANNOY ME BY EXISTING

JUNIPER LEWIS

ACKNOWLEDGEMENTS

I can't say your names, because I don't want you to be associated with my own political choices. But I hope that one day you will know who you are.

CONTENTS

INTRODUCTION

I had to write this book because I am fed up with the way things are going in this country. At every turn, it seems as though more and more of us are being oppressed, marginalized, or otherwise silenced. We're forced to make our point on signs during marches rather than being given a seat at the table that people in privileged majorities have enjoyed since time immemorial. It's time to air our grievances in one of the few truly powerful forms of communication to which we currently have access: the written word.

Many ideas in this book are going to upset a lot of people. I can't avoid it. I am a person of color who has just had enough. I stress the importance of calling people by their proper pronouns, but every time I ask someone to utilize a modicum of respect and call people by their chosen pronouns, I am met with eye rolls from those who just do not understand our struggle. Sadly, my fight is not unique. America in 2018 is a more chaotic place with more animus toward minorities than at any other time since the civil rights movement.

This book is going to seem like one long rant, because in many ways it is. This book is less about statistics and data than it is about experience and wisdom. I've gained this wisdom by experiencing live as a member of several different historically oppressed social groups.

I have never known what it means to truly belong to the majority. I feel incredibly unsafe in this world, and I know that millions of other people feel the same way. I needed a place to unleash my feelings. I needed a safe space. Unfortunately, the blank page is one of the few places that I can truly express myself without fear of retribution. I can be honest here.

The plight of people of color is just one among many other significant acts of discrimination that American society has created, specifically through the actions of Republicans. From income inequality to lack of accessible health care, it seems as though this country has it out for citizens that do not fall into a relatively narrow band of social qualifications. Simply put, if you're not a straight, white male, it's incredibly hard to truly succeed in this country. And it's not our fault. We're constantly told that we can succeed if we work hard. Yet so many black children live their lives somewhere in the school to prison pipeline. We are saddled with student loan debt in order to climb just one rung of the social ladder that gets longer and longer each year. How can we ever expect to get ahead when the path to success is changed and the rules of prosperity are broken and redefined almost every day?

This book is not an argument. It is an indictment and a cry for help. I'm examining the current system we live in and attempting to demonstrate that it has committed unspeakable crimes against people like me and countless others who don't look or act "the right way". Specifically, I'm looking at the way that American Republicans have set these horrible chains of events into action. Apart from exposing the system for what it is, I'm really just asking for a little bit of help. Don't pity the rich man and cut his taxes so that he can buy another yacht. Use the resources that we all helped him accumulate through collective hard work and societal opportunity to instead bolster the very community that created him. Yes, he works hard, but so do the rest of us. Give us some credit instead of separating us from the ultra-rich more and more every day.

I just want the boot of oppression lifted from our necks. Just when we thought we had legitimate representation in the person of the first black president, we go and elect a notable bigot to lead the "free world". Is this country supposed to feel safe for everyone who lives in it? Do we believe that all men are created equal, as the Founding Fathers told us? It seems that fewer people than ever actually believe this maxim. How can we live our lives without having to constantly look over our shoulders for the next white supremacist or hate crime? This is something that white America just does not understand. They would rather spend time and effort decrying a simple protest of the national anthem than actually standing up and attempting to solve the problem. I guess it's easier to deny an issue exists than to devise a remedy.

I know this all seems scattered and angry, but that's exactly how I feel. I don't have all the answers, but I think I have a few. This book is an attempt to try to put all of those things in one place. It's not a sociological tome and it's not an economics textbook. You won't see graphs or charts. What you will see is a perspective that I believe is shared by a sizable minority of the American people. All I can hope is that what I'm saying makes sense to those of you out there who feel that you do not have a voice. If you feel that your country has let you down and that you have committed yourself to forming whatever resistance you can to the current state of oppression, this book is for you. If you disagree with the principles I espouse in this book, then I'm sorry. But you may just be part of the problem, and you likely annoy me by existing.

1
———

TRUMP

I should begin with a discussion of our president. Really, this book would not be possible without the man himself, our forty-fifth president (somehow), Mr. Donald J. Trump. Before Trump, I simply co-existed with Republicans, hoping that they had a soul lingering under a surface of oppression of minorities and demanding to control how women utilize their reproductive faculties. I honestly believed that we all wanted to improve the country, but that we had genuine disagreements about how to do it. Then Trump came along.

This is a man whose election irrevocably changed the course of American history in countless ways. One day, he was considered a pipe dream of his own design, a figment of his own megalomania. The next, he stood at a podium and declared victory over Hillary Clinton, a woman whose experience and poised promised to continue the trail of greatness that Barack Obama started with his monumental election in 2008. The pendulum has swung fully in the opposite direction.

Unlike with a real pendulum, the two sides between which our politics seems to swing are not equal. One side hearkens back to a mythical time when America was "great". While America did possess a great deal of wealth and influence during this time, it also waged a campaign against anyone who could not honestly check a certain class of boxes. Those who were not straight, white, and male were destined to second-class status. The latter half of the twentieth century was dedicated to righting these wrongs and electing candidates who could ensure that we did not regress as a society.

Donald Trump's very existence as a political figure threatened to set us back decades if not centuries. He was never shy about informing us of this fact through a series of caustic tweets and inflammatory speeches designed to stir up a specific group of people. He has always been the candidate and representative of the "oppressed" white male. These privileged men have sworn themselves to victimhood, and yearn to keep everyone who does not look like them relegated to the back of the proverbial bus. Meanwhile, an age of progress hangs in the balance.

The 2008 recession spawned an entire generation of white men who believed that their unearned prosperity was being ripped away from them by advancements in technology and the rise of prominent minority leadership figures. Their cushy factory jobs were being replaced by machines and affirmative action limited the slots available to them in institutions of higher education. They blamed progress and brown people for their lack of ability to advance in society, and they lashed out in greater and greater numbers. The dogma of personal responsibility and accountability somehow did not apply to them.

But progress always stopped their numbers from growing into unwieldy masses. Barack Obama stood up and promised to protect us from those forces that conspired to take us back to the era of Jim Crow and opposition to female suffrage. But as quickly as the candle of his inspiration was lit, the flames of oppression helped forge a strong metal snuffer to put out that fire and cast us all back into darkness. That candle snuffer had a name: Donald Trump.

Trump knew what it took to get elected. He knew that a businessman with no political experience would face an uphill battle from the very beginning. In order to win an election, he had to convince people to vote for him. Since he had no experience or discernible political savvy, he had to appeal to a base of disgruntled white male voters who believed that something had been taken away from them by uppity brown people who had the audacity to strive for more in this world. He also needed to persuade their wives to vote against their own best interests and follow the big white man who would just as soon grab them by the genitals while their husbands looked the other way.

Luckily for Trump, these myopic fellows were in great supply. While Hillary Clinton campaigned along the coasts and some of the big cities in the Midwest, Trump focused on galvanizing his base everywhere else. He schlepped from small rust belt town to small rust belt town, carrying a basket of lies and racism designed to give white people hope. He promised to deport the illegal immigrants that were supposedly responsible for taking jobs meant for middle Americans, despite the fact that middle America paid great sums to invest in technology to avoid doing those kinds of jobs. He promised to bring back the factory jobs that had either been automated or shipped overseas. All he asked for was a vote.

In order to play to the cognitive dissonance present in the minds of rich and middle-class white people, Trump could not act overtly racist. He had to cloak his bigotry under a thin fabric of lip service to unity and the American dream. If you took him at his word, Trump wanted everyone to succeed. There was room in his America for everyone to thrive. Meanwhile anyone who could read between the lines knew that he was actually promising to work behind the scenes to bolster the very forces that have oppressed women and minorities for generations.

If you think about it, his approach makes a lot of sense if your ultimate goal is to increase the social standing of the rich, white man in America. The real power structures that keep women and minorities down come from the ability of corporations to continue their business activities unabated. Trump understood this better than anyone, since he profited from generations of business experience and wealth. He earned very little on his own, but envisioned himself as the epitome of the American dream.

If corporations can do what they want without interference from the government, the situation will naturally shake out to increase oppression of women and people of color. Decreasing social mobility is easy when one group of people holds most of the cards. If you eliminate minimum wage laws, you can guarantee that poor people are unable to rub two nickels together and get a loaf of bread, let alone accrue any real wealth. Since most poor people tend to be people of color due to our country's painful history, the logic follows rather easily. If banks can engage in risky activity while keeping their profits private and pushing their losses onto the American people in the form of bailouts, poor people eat all the detriments and reap none of the gains. It's a perfect system if you are a rich, white man.

Trump offered all this and more to the American populace, and we put diametrically opposed ideologies to a referendum. Democrats felt confident in their so-called "blue wall", and took the election largely for granted. Hillary promised to, for the most part, continue the policies of President Obama and usher in a greater era of progress and prosperity. Trump, it appeared to everyone with a brain, threatened to scuttle the ship and distribute lifeboats to people based on wealth and skin color. The stakes of the election could not have been made more clear, and Americans went to the polls with this knowledge.

The blue wall ultimately crumbled as Trump wrenched crucial bricks from its foundation. The American people spoke in two ways. True democracy proved itself to be in favor of progress, as Hillary overwhelmingly won the popular vote. If we lived in an actual democracy instead of a jerry-rigged assembly of states subject to the antiquated structure known as the electoral college, we would all be in a better place right now. Keep in mind, the electoral college was designed to ensure that the people could not directly elect the president.

And, so, here we are. Conservative whites continue to sing Trump's praises as policy after policy is enacted to ensure their long term prosperity. Meanwhile, there is the pesky issue of the our existence. Every day, the establishment adds insult to injury by pretending that minorities are doing better than they ever have. All the while, we fear being shot by a cop having a bad day, losing our jobs for discussing issues of inequality, and continuing to hand more money to the wealthy by way of tax cuts.

This is why Republicans annoy me, as your could have guessed, simply by existing. It's easy to pretend that things are going well when you can hide from the storm in your shelter of privilege. Republicans already carried the mantle of stepping on the poor and helping the rich, but now they have added to that mantle the active oppression of women and minorities. Using their better faculties, most Republicans actually vehemently opposed Donald Trump as a candidate before he secured the Republican nomination in 2016. They knew what would ultimately come from a Trump presidency. But once he secured the nomination, they realized that their collective political fate depended on this petulant man-child. I'd feel bad if they were otherwise good people. But they're not, so I don't.

Trump has lived up to all expectations, and then some. He began by immediately seeking to dismantle the Affordable Care Act, a hallmark piece of Obama-era legislation. In doing so, he actively stood against the right of all Americans to receive quality health care, regardless of their social or financial situation. What a surprise! He doesn't care about the health of the American people. To him, health care is all about dollars and cents, as opposed to the well-being of people who desire to live a good life. Even Republicans could not get on board with destroying the ACA without a replacement. They knew that they could not get reelected if they voted for such a disastrous repeal plan. I'll talk more about health care later, but make no mistake. Our current health care disaster has Trump's name all over it, just like every ghastly building he has ever commissioned. At least it's not as tacky and gaudy as the Trump Taj Mahal.

So Trump moved on and appealed to deeper conservative sensibilities. Even the Republican desire to strip health care from the poor has a limit. But if you want to appeal to a potential voter group, appeal to their pocketbooks. Tax cuts were the natural next step for guaranteeing Trump's popularity among conservative white men in America. It's as if these people were not already the beneficiaries of centuries of racist and oppressive policies designed to benefit white men at the expense of literally everyone else. Trump's tax plan overtly favored the rich, eroding the few remaining taxes that put a mild strain on their balance sheets. He was repaying the debt that he owed corporate America by speaking to their sensibilities in order to help him win the election.

The stock market soared as a result, and he took credit for every single point added to the Dow Jones Industrial Average. Trump believed that the stock market was a referendum on the early stages of his presidency, and that he was coming out ahead. He paid no attention to the fact that the middle class continued to diminish and that wages continued to stagnate. Wealthy people were happy, and that's all that mattered. What did it matter to him that government revenues were slashed while trillions of dollars remained on the books, committed to be spent for various government programs?

All the while, he tweeted. Conservatives insisted upon focusing on his policies rather than his words, as if words don't matter. Our standing on the world stage has almost never been worse. His racist, bigoted, myopic tweets poison any potential good that could ever come out of his presidency (as if there were any). But why are we surprised? This is the man who told us that Mexico was bringing rapists and murderers, adding to an already toxic perception of Latin@s in this country. This is the man who openly bragged about being able to grab women by the genitals after meeting them. This is the man who settled lawsuit after lawsuit that could have tainted his presidential image.

This president is a pathogen in the bloodstream of the collective American body. We have to fight back or else we risk being overcome. Even antibiotics are only effective if they are administered before an illness has advanced too far. We have the most powerful cure at our disposal in our ability to take collective action and fill the airwaves with the sounds of our protest. The internet has made protest more visible than ever before. It can be done. But we have to get started before it is too late.

~

THE TIME for dialogue has long passed. Dialogue is for debates on issues like fuel taxes and local millages. We can engage in meaningful discussion on matters of philosophy and worldview, which is why elections prove to be one of the most fruitful times for political conversation. But we no longer have time to talk through these issues. If you have time, you have privilege. The rest of us are suffering at the hands of a man who is taking our rights away one by one each and every day he occupies the Oval Office.

We can no longer afford to take any prisoners. This is the fault of Republicans and we have to start acting like it. If you have loved ones who fall into this camp, you have to let them know of your opposition to the very fabric of their worldview. You owe it to yourself and everyone who depends on the advancement of progress in this country. I certainly do not advocate destroying friendships or familial ties. But at the same time, there is no room for anyone to sit on the sidelines. You're either with us, or you're against us.

Luckily, we people of color can count more white people among our allies than at any other point in history. Your advocacy for our rights and our personhood cannot be understated or under- appreciated. But we need more. We have been told for too long that we are behaving like victims and that white people are no longer responsible for our suffering. This, of course, happens while rich white men plot ways to become richer at the expense of the poor and people of color. White people, you have a place in this fight, too. If, somehow, you lose some aspect of your privilege, you become subject to the same forces to which we have been made to submit for generations. Come struggle and fight with us. There's more than enough room in the tent.

2

RACE

I thought it only fair to start off with the real elephant in the room. You see stories about it all over the news every day, which may just be an indicator that people are starting to care about it. That's right, I'm talking about racism. I'm talking about the reason that I have to be cautious in all of my daily interactions, lest I end up another statistic splattered all over a central Missouri sidewalk, torn apart by the bullets of another uncaring cop's gun. Racial minorities in this country have it incredibly hard, and I don't think that most people truly understand the anger and disappointment that we feel each and every day.

Let's start with just the issue of police brutality. From Michael Brown to Eric Garner, black people in this country have been shown time and time again that our lives mean less than those of white people. This is not debatable. If a cop killed some white woman named Becky, the flags would be flown at half mast and we would have meaningful legislative change regarding police violence tomorrow. But our black skin shields us from expecting any real change in this arena. Instead we condition ourselves to anticipate sadness and desperation, and all we can do is hope that the violence will somehow spare us and our children. This becomes something of a selfish and loathsome thought, because we know that if it skips us, it will affect someone else.

White people just cannot understand what it means to be a black person in America. They can't put themselves in the shoes of Eric Garner, who was strangled to death in the middle of a sidewalk in broad daylight just because he happened to sell a few loose cigarettes. The story of Michael Brown sent white people running to the internet to justify his killing. They turned theft into a capital offense, condemning him due to his alleged taking of cigarillos from a gas station. Why was this easier than admitting we have a problem? That wouldn't have even required any work. All it would have taken is an admission that white people have it easier when it comes to interacting with the police. But admitting that you have an advantage is a painful process for so many people, it comes as no surprise that white people were unwilling to do so even when faced with the tears of mothers burying their children.

So black people decided to take matters into their own hands. After being told by society that our lives are worth less than those of white people, we made our own group to fight back against that narrative. We gave it a title that reflected our simple philosophy on this issue: Black Lives Matter. This was hardly a controversial assertion. But immediately the evil right pounced on us like the panthers they so feared that we would become. A counter-narrative emerged, telling us that "All Lives Matter" and "Blue Lives Matter". They tried to portray black people as an ungrateful and uncivilized mass trying to put itself above the rest of society as white people have done for generations. They couldn't have us threatening their power. Instead, they hung an entire counter-movement on the absence of one word in our movement. Would it really have made that much of a difference if we had called our group "Black Lives Matter, <u>Too</u>"? I somehow doubt it.

We marched in the streets and did everything we could to tell people that our minds and our bodies were worth something. Being descendants of slaves, we were used to fighting back against those who sought to use us for something other than what we want. This fight was nothing new. We rallied around our own and sought to hold politicians accountable for their stance on an issue that literally meant life or death for our community. What else could anyone be expected to do under the circumstances? They slaughtered us like cattle and expect us to line up in front of the slaughterhouse. Yet at every turn, they mocked us for stepping out of the death march. They called us terrorists for asserting our basic rights and refused to march with us. It's as though they learned nothing from King.

Like so many fights before, we were prepared to go it alone, without support from other communities. What's more, we were prepared to struggle against the powerful majority that plotted to keep us down at every turn. All we could do was bring awareness to an issue and show that we were truly the victims of forces much more powerful than they have ever allowed us to be. But white people did what they always do. They told us to suck it up. They told us to make something of ourselves, to dress better and speak better so that we would have to worry less about running afoul of the police. I thought the police were the ones who wore uniforms in order to show that they protect and serve. But now we have to wear a suit just to avoid being killed.

Black Lives Matter gained traction, and the threat to white power became greater and greater. As more and more powerful black people began to sign on to our message, it became clear to white people that they couldn't let this continue unabated. So they began to attack the powerful black people in the arenas that had defined their success. In certain cases, this happened in literal arenas as black people were demonized for having the audacity to kneel for the national anthem. They had to manufacture patriotism just to get people to pay attention to their evil counter-narrative. Nobody cared about standing for the national anthem before those protests. But because black knees were touching the field during the precious anthem, it became an affront to their newly-created values.

The halls of power took their side and put pressure on businesses to stifle the expression of black athletes. The president openly tweeted against black Americans standing up for what they thought was right. How embarrassing is it to know that Trump took the side of a song over the lives of black people who were being killed in the streets? That was exactly what we were trying to tell people. Black Lives Matter, certainly more than a song. Apparently some people still need convincing. Black athletes had their livelihoods threatened, and in one instance actually taken away. Fans and powerful businessmen agreed that certain players did not deserve to play because of their political beliefs, and they took away a man's way of earning a living. All of this, of course, was because he took a knee. He didn't burn a flag. He took a knee during a song. What an act.

That's where we stand. Black Lives still do not Matter to white people. Police shootings continue in this country, with the perpetrators largely never seeing an indictment, let alone a conviction by a jury of their peers. We are in the midst of a referendum on the true value of black lives and black bodies in this country, and we are losing badly. The measure is being defeated.

3

IMMIGRATION

Our immigration system is broken. Millions of poor, hardworking souls from other countries try feebly to make a better life for themselves and their families. All we do is turn a blind eye. The current administration has made a mockery of everything it means to be a human, let alone an American. We used to let people into our country by the boatload. Our grandparents and great-grandparents had a relatively easy time becoming citizens. Often, all they would have to do is accept a name change in exchange for admission to a country with vast and bountiful resources.

Who are we if we forget our past? We are the descendants of immigrants, all of us. At the very least, many of us come from a lineage of rapists and murderers who took everything Native Americans had and manifestly called it their destiny. Some of us, myself included, come from those who were brought here in chains, fated to work for nothing and grind our bones to dust against our will in pursuit of gain for our kidnappers. In any event, few of us can really claim any significant "right" to be present in the United States. Only Native Americans have a real case to present.

We have turned into a nation that prides itself on shunning brown people in the name of patriotism. Our newspapers simultaneously deride the honest aims of people attempting to better their lot in life while advertising that we have more jobs available than we have people to fill them. American immigration policy is the functional equivalent of laughing at a poor person while choking a little bit on a mouth full of food. We suffer, but we have not yet felt the pangs of our karma. We deserve worse, and I honestly believe we will get it once our places of employment become empty after the last ICE raid.

You never hear stories about illegal white immigrants on the news. By all accounts, you would almost think they don't exist. But the truth is that our system is set out to make sure that poor people and people of color suffer. We've become a well-oiled machine of exploitation, and brown and black bodies serve as our fuel. The pistons churn, and our exhaust pipes spit out the dark black smoke of imprisoned children and separated families. We all choke on the products of our heinous crimes and pretend that we can see through the haze. What is wrong with us?

I had some faith that true dialogue could be had in this country until I saw those children locked up behind that steel gray fencing. The images hearkened back to the Japanese internment camps, another ingenious American idea. What had these children done to deserve being separated from their parents? Their parents committed a misdemeanor, just like millions of drunk drivers on our roads. Yet their families were fractured while the inebriated hedge fund manager cut a deal using a fancy lawyer and made it home in time for dinner.

But the time for discussion is over. One cannot reasonably converse with someone who thinks this treatment of children is anything remotely resembling acceptable. This is barbarism, plain and simple. It is coldly and carefully constructed oppression, manufactured by your friendly neighborhood Republican. They did this. Our resistance means nothing if it does not start with this black and white issue. Make no mistake, the Republican party engineered the mass imprisonment of brown children in order to maintain some perverse notion of "patriotism".

Think about it. Black athletes are continually demonized for having the audacity to kneel during the national anthem while children from Mexico and Central America are thrown into cages like animals. Their cries mean less than the cries of fat, rich, white men who wail at the image of a black athlete showing any sort of protest toward a country that has oppressed him and his people for hundreds of years. That should tell you where their priorities really stand. But then again, it's not their child staring down the barrel of a life without their parents. It's not their children who thought they might have better life by virtue of their parents escaping gang-run cities and extreme violence in their hometowns. Their kids just have to deal with designer drugs and clandestine overdoses. What a hard life they must lead.

Trump couldn't even undo his own horror the right way. When the American people began to stand up and voice their opposition to children being held in literal cages, he cried uncle. But his version of crying uncle is going back to a milder version of his own heinous crimes. He still stuck with his unspeakable "zero tolerance" policy toward illegal immigration, but he allowed families to be detained together. That's the political equivalent of being thrown from a fire into a frying pan. We still have imprisoned children! The children are still behind bars! What don't people understand about this? No matter which way you slice it or dice it, children are still growing up behind bars because their parents committed a misdemeanor.

A true liberal candidate would have never allowed this to happen. A real leftist would recognize that a positive future does not dictate rigidly enforcing arbitrary lines drawn on maps. That person would likely realize that we are one global family and that all of us are mutually dependent on each other for survival in some way or another. Immigrants have helped our country in so many different ways. Intellectually, immigrants have provided some of our greatest scientific, philosophical, and legal advances. Physically, immigrants have formed the backbone of our agricultural system for as long as they have been here. Spiritually, immigrants have become some of the most ardent activists for humanitarian causes, likely because they have seen and borne the brunt of the worst that humanity has to offer.

The main problem with liberals is that we have not done enough to oppose these oppressive regimes and policies. We have seen time and again that true revolution is the only way to enact real change. The time has come to put our money where our mouth is. Republicans clamor after the lives of "unborn children". Well, it's about time that we clamor after the lives of children who have been born, locked in cages, and told that they matter less than someone who was fortunate enough to be born on American soil. Rather than allowing the mainstream Republican anti-immigration message to permeate our culture, we need to stand up for our brothers and sisters who were born abroad. We need to let them know that they are just as welcome here as we are. We just have to take out the trash during our election cycle so that they will be able to stay here and make a life.

If you voted for Trump, you voted for this. The anguish and torment that those children experience each and every day are on your hands, and I hope it eats away at you day and night. Even if it does, you are only experiencing a mere fraction of what those children had to go through after being ripped from the arms of their parents. You voted for discrimination. You voted for hatred. I don't care how much you say you voted for the future of your country or that you voted against politics as usual. He made himself clear from the get-go that he was going to do something like this. It was only because of our overwhelmingly loud voices that he even backed down as much as he did. We clearly make an impression. We just can't tire out at this point. The kids are depending on us.

I ask you, Republicans, what are immigrants even doing to you? How are you suffering due to the "surge" in illegal immigration? Don't give me some spiel about taxes. My tax money goes to pay for your precious military that gets sent all over the world to destabilize regions and create refugee crises. I want to know what your real gripe is with these people. Would you not do anything you could to ensure that your children could have better life than you did? Isn't that the entire point of being a parent? Isn't that the entire point of societal advancement? Most of us have it better than our parents did, and that is due in large part to the fact that we actually let people engage in the honest pursuit of life, liberty, and happiness. So, what is the problem?

I think I know what the issue is. These people don't look like you. Face it, Republicans. You are overwhelmingly white and xenophobic. These two characteristics are hardly coincidentally located within the same group of people. You just can't stand the idea of brown people making a better life for themselves alongside your family that has been in this country for generations. In your mind, you've earned something. What have you earned? You had no choice in determining where you were born. You got lucky, but you refuse to lend a helping hand to those people who are just trying to create their own luck in this world.

So what do you want to do? You want to build a wall to keep these people out of the country. I thought you hated taxes. But it's fine to spend as much money as necessary to make sure that people don't cross that precious border of yours. You Republicans really do make me sick. You stick to your principles except when it comes to actually making a difference in the world or improving the lives of people who have a different skin color than you do. Put yourself in their shoes for a second. Imagine that someone ripped your kids from your arms and threw them in prison, while dragging you to a different prison. You would likely never see your child again. Surely, you can't think that's a good thing.

But you would never cross a border illegally. You're a decent, law-abiding American. You've never been convicted of a crime, and you likely never will be. You would never do something so indecent and unthinkable as cross an invisible line to save your family, would you? You wouldn't do that, of course, unless you were put in a situation where you needed to do just that. Well, guess what. These people have been faced with an unthinkable situation. They are fleeing gangs and drug dealers in order to make sure that their families do not have to live with the risk of violence and harm that comes with living in their hometowns.

Republicans serve as a dam against the natural stream of immigrants that powers the turbines of growth and progress in this country. These people are not stealing anyone's job. They are taking the jobs that Americans feel that they are too good to do. Traditional conservative ideals value hard work and the American dream. The concept of the American dream has its roots in the rags-to-riches narrative. Yet, Republicans want to keep immigrants in rags and deny them any opportunity to achieve riches. They continue to push the idea of "obtaining citizenship the right way" while ignoring the reality that many of these people need to escape dire circumstances **now**.

In reality, Republicans push the "obtaining citizenship the right way" schtick in order to kick the can down the road and ensure that they don't actually have to seem like jerks when they advocate for policies that result in children being locked in cages. It's a way to glorify the "hardworking legal immigrant" at the expense of the person who doesn't have the money or time to interact with the laborious set of regulations and laws surrounding immigration to the United States. Republicans claim to be against regulations that impact the right of people to do what they want, so long as it's not at the expense of others. I guess they're not willing to extend their own arguments to their logical conclusion when the lives and welfare of brown people are at issue.

But then again, what can we expect from people who vote for a man who says that immigration is bringing "rapists and murderers" as opposed to the candidate who recognizes that immigration spurs progress and innovation? This is going to get worse before it gets better, and it's up to us to make sure that we cut it off where it really counts. Vote against the people who would rather see children locked in cells screaming for their parents than see a black man kneel for a song. This shouldn't even need explaining, but for some reason it still does. These people want to turn the car of history around and force us off a cliff. We can't let that happen. We won't let it happen.

4

THE RICH

America has long been an oligarchy, a society governed by relatively few rich and powerful individuals. Every day, the influence of the rich grows and the mobility of the poor and middle class diminishes. It's important to explore exactly what the place of rich people is in American society and whether it makes sense to continue with the current paradigm.

It would be silly to say that rich people are evil or that being rich is undesirable. None of us would work as hard as we do or come up with creative ideas to improve our lives if we didn't hope to ultimately become wealthy as a result of our efforts. However, rich people are not a monolith and wealth is not a proxy of virtue.

Rich people are not better than poor people. Without understanding this basic tenet, further conversation cannot be had on the topic. Rich people are not necessarily smarter, harder-working, more special, or more unique than people of limited means. More often than not, wealth comes as a combination of advantage, luck, and hard work. Different people adjust the dials in various ways in order to reach their goal, but very few people become affluent without checking all three boxes.

Two of these aspects of wealth are not earned. Advantage is not earned. People of certain demographics are just more likely to earn significant amounts of money in their lifetime. These demographics are typically white, abled (not suffering from a disability), male, straight, and coming from a financially privileged background, among others. None of these characteristics can be earned by the individual who benefits from them. As a result, one cannot take credit for wealth insofar as one has benefited from being in one or more of these categories.

Further, luck cannot be earned. How many people have stumbled into wealth simply by doing the right thing at the right time? They certainly deserve credit for doing the thing itself. But they largely are not in charge of the proper timing to engage in their enterprise. Further, whether people will be receptive to a certain idea or product largely cannot be predicted. Markets forces dictate profitability. Even if we assume that advantage, luck, and hard work are present in equal quantities in a given wealthy person's situation, it stands to reason that two-thirds of a wealthy person's success is not earned.

But we live in a society where rich people are considered to be special simply by virtue of having a great deal of money. That's why people think Donald Trump is somehow unique. However, the combination of his advantage and luck far outweighs the two-thirds figure I presented above. Because rich people hold so many of the cards in America, they disproportionately control the way that the rest of us live our lives. In many cases, it is important to make sure that rich people are accountable to the rest of us, for most of them would not be wealthy without us in the first place.

Liberal politicians have famously reminded business owners who claimed to be self-made or otherwise unique that others were involved in their success. They made us remember that businesses usually sit on roads that are publicly funded, depend on workers who are often critically underpaid, and are formed through the sweat and toil of employees who get no ownership in what they helped to build. In short, rich people usually didn't get where they are on their own, yet they enjoy the lion's share of the success of their projects. In order to set the record straight, it is important to put checks on wealth.

The most important and obvious check on wealth is taxation. Taxes on the rich have been critically low for far too long. The top marginal tax rate in the United States was once far higher than it is now. Now it is criminally low. In order to make rich people aware that they live in the same community as the rest of us, they must be made to contribute to the collective goods of that community. I'll talk more about income inequality specifically in a later chapter.

Beyond taxes, rich people need to be reigned in by adequate regulations on industry. The richest of the rich obtained their wealth by innovating in a particular industry. Many of the products that you and I use on a daily basis come from these innovations and the companies that were created to distribute them. However, these companies have wrought unspeakable public harm in pursuit of further profit for their shareholders. From environmental disasters to underpaying workers, there is no end to what the rich will do to get richer. In order to ensure that our interests are adequately balanced against the interests of the rich, regulation must be increased to keep industry in its proper place.

But perhaps the greatest change that must come if we are to wrest control of America back from the claws of the greedy one percent is a broad change in the way the rich are perceived. If we stop looking at rich people as being somehow special or gifted and simply look at them as people who have greater resources, then we will be less likely to grant them the power they so crave. If riches didn't come with power and influence, it is far less likely that people would put financial prosperity above more important things in live like love and fellowship.

There's no reason why American society should be content with the extreme levels of wealth that we see at the top ends of income distribution charts. I'm not talking about millionaires, or even ten-digit billionaires. I really mean eleven or twelve-digit billionaires. The fact that this kind of money can find itself into the hands of a single person is a symptom of a much larger social problem. Greed must be contained, and we as a collective have the ability to contain it by electing politicians who will make it a priority to ensure that all Americans benefit from our collective wealth.

Charity, while admirable, is not enough to ensure that the rich do their fair share in helping to prop up the country that helped to make them who they are. Unfortunately, this assistance must be forced. To the extent that people oppose law and regulation that seeks to make these goals into realities, they really intend to spit in the face of those who are truly suffering in this country. People who claim to be self-made ignore the people who put them on their shoulders and helped them to the mountaintop. It is truly a disgusting attitude to have.

Luckily, many millionaires and billionaires in this country espouse these values. Countless liberal entertainers and business-people advocate for higher taxes and checks on rich people despite the fact that this works against their own best interests on paper. Our opposition lives in the heart of those who cling to their wealth with greedy, cold hands and refuse to give even an iota of their wealth to help make this country a better place. This attitude borders on pure evil in and of itself, and we must make it our mission to keep it from dominating our politics and our national ethos.

Campaign finance reform is another crucial step in keeping greedy rich people from tightening their grip on the American people. *Citizens United* opened the door for the rich to dictate who gets elected and what policy ultimately becomes law. That decision is the linchpin to guaranteeing that our democracy remains pure and that our society remains free. This is why elections matter. In order to get that decision reversed, we must vote for presidents who will appoint justices who will ultimately vote to overrule it at the first opportunity. Actions like these help to keep the rich in check and make sure that the middle and lower classes are adequately represented in American politics. Democratic and leftist candidates have made this part of their platform, and it is important that we continue to support them.

It is also important to note that not all rich people fall into the category of wealthy individuals whose influence must be curtailed. It would be difficult to say that our cherished movie stars and musicians are greedy despite the fact that they champion causes of equality and protection for women and minorities. If you're rich, and you espouse the principles I've laid out in this chapter, please know that I'm not talking about you. Keep doing what you're doing. You may be our only hope in the long run.

But if you fall into the other category of rich people, please know that people like me will not stand idly by as you continue to poison our country and its politics. You had the opportunity to use your wealth and influence for good, but instead you have chosen to use it to work against the welfare and livelihood of the rest of us. Realistically, you can't expect us to take this lying down. The Occupy Wall Street movement was a great starting place, but we have much more up our collective sleeve, and we are more united than we have ever been.

Rich people need everyone else in order to succeed. Giant companies are only as big as the number of people who work for them. If we all turn against the insanely rich people who insist on holding everyone else down, their wealth vanishes quick. I don't hate rich people, but I do hate what riches can do to otherwise good people. Just as rich people often work hard to ensure that their interests are protected, please know that I and everyone else I can convince of the need to put a check on the influence of the rich will fight to protect our own. I can't guarantee victory, but I can say that it will be a hell of a fight.

5

―――――

THE WAR ON DRUGS

I f Republicans have exhibited greater hypocrisy with respect to a given issue than they have on drug laws, I have yet to see it. Most, but certainly not all, Republican stances are internally consistent, even if they are reprehensible as a whole. But having a war on drugs makes no sense even under a Republican worldview. Generally, conservatives advocate for individual rights and liberties while viewing government restriction on individual action with a certain amount of skepticism. Of course, there exist exceptions to this line of thinking. (See, the abortion debate generally.)

However, even when Republicans recognize an exception to the general maxim that individual liberties are to be favored over government's ability to restrain people, there is generally some greater societal harm that they are seeking to avoid. They want to ban abortions because they believe fetuses are people. They want to increase government surveillance because they think that certain individuals present a threat to national security. There is room for debate there, but the arguments make some sense even if the underlying ideology is flawed.

But the Republican stance on drug restriction makes absolutely no sense, particularly when it comes to marijuana. Drug use is an issue that affects the individual and only the individual. To the extent that the effects of drug use harm others, laws are already in place to address those negative impacts. Drinking and driving is already a crime even though alcohol is legal to consume for those over twenty-one years of age. Crimes surrounding drug use will continue to occur whether a given drug is legal or not, and the laws banning those crimes will continue to be enforced.

Imagine that heroin is legalized tomorrow. Of course, you would still see heroin addicts like you do today, except they would be free instead of rotting in prison for drug use and possession. If the addict keeps using and his addiction worsens, that is his own business. He has to pay the price for his own choices. However, if the addict starts stealing in order to fund his addiction, he will be arrested for theft. If he gets to the point that he begins beating his wife, he will go to jail for assault and domestic violence. If he drives while under the influence of heroin, he will be arrested for driving under the influence of a narcotic. All of this is true whether or not heroin is legalized.

The same remains true of all other drugs. Yet we retain an active war on drugs due to the machinations of previous Republican presidential administrations. This war has filled American prisons with nonviolent drug offenders, particularly people of color. All the while, the taxpayer bears the brunt of these atrocious policies. You would think that between a combination of advocacy for individual liberties and an appeal to the financial stress placed on the taxpayer, Republicans would be the first ones aboard the drug legalization train. But for some reason, they keep pushing for the punishment of nonviolent drug offenders without regard to the size of the bill that will be passed on to the American tax base.

This contradiction has become more glaring in 2018 than at any other point in American history. With an opioid crisis in full swing and a meth epidemic that continues to rage on in economically depressed areas of the country, Republicans offer no solutions other than imprisoning those who suffer from addictions to these substances. Worse yet, conservatives advocate for tax breaks and corporate welfare on behalf of the pharmaceutical companies that distribute opioids and make billions of dollars of profit off of the addiction and pain of those who have been prescribed these drugs. If it seems evil on the surface, it's because you're perceptive.

But let's assume the truth of one point of the Republican argument concerning the war on drugs, which is the following: There is some societal harm that comes from drug use in and of itself, and we need a law to address drug possession and use for that reason. This is a preposterous assumption, as there are countless individuals across all industries who succeed in life despite recreational drug use. But just for a minute, let's grant their point. If that's the case, what good comes from throwing drug users in prison? Even if we grant the proposition that the law should ban drug possession and use, why not just seize drugs when they are found and/or impose fines on drug users?

There is no reason to tear families apart by throwing people in cages for using drugs. Prisons destroy individuals and change family trees for generations. They should be reserved for the worst of the worst in society. I'm talking about murderers, rapists, terrorists and the like. Single fathers who use marijuana to relax after a long day at work should not have to fear being ripped from their children for simply trying to enjoy themselves. If you really care about the liberty of the individual, you should have no desire to jail people for putting something in their body. It's their body, it's their choice. But Republicans have shown time and time again that they want to control people's choices regarding their own bodies.

So what is the real reason that Republicans continue the war on drugs and persist in filling prisons with those evil drug users? The answer is fairly simple. Republicans want to wage a war on the lower class and minorities. They want to punish those demographics by any means necessary, and the war on drugs is a very easy way to achieve that goal. That desire is even easier to fulfill if you enforce drug laws unevenly across communities. There's a reason that most nonviolent drug offenders in America's prisons are people of color. It's not because people of color are inherently more likely to use drugs than white people. It's because black people caught with drugs are far more likely to receive harsh sentences than white people caught with the same drugs in the same circumstances.

Why are we surprised? Almost every Republican policy has an incredibly bigoted or racist rationale behind it. Think about a white high-schooler who is caught with a joint in his backpack. Do you really think that kid is going to prison? At worst, he's going to get a lecture from his school's guidance counselor, and he'll probably end up smoking the joint with his dad on the back porch at the end of the night. A black kid in the same situation is probably going to be put through the criminal justice system and will be released with a warning if he's very lucky. White kids are taught how to avoid being caught with drugs while black kids are taught that they will lose their freedom if they are caught with even the most innocuous of drugs.

Perhaps the clearest test case of the despicable Republican stance on this issue is the continued Republican opposition to statutes legalizing marijuana use. Marijuana is probably about as safe as alcohol, if not more so. Several states across the country have legalized marijuana through their own referenda, and that number will continue to grow. But Republicans refuse to come out for the legalization of marijuana as a whole. Why do you think that is? Do you think Republicans have an actual, ideological opposition to marijuana use in and of itself? Or are they opposed to legalizing marijuana because it is a drug that has historically been associated with brown and black people? We all know the answer.

They've all seen movies where the hip, cool, black dude smokes a joint. But Republicans don't want their kids to wind up like those black dudes. You can just see the fear in their eyes. So what is the most logical way to keep that from happening, in their eyes? Keep marijuana illegal and continue to enact criminal penalties for its possession and use. That's the easiest way to punish black people for having the gall to use pot. Anything that goes against that paradigm goes against the way that they think people should behave. Substances associated with blackness or brownness should be illegal, and the penalties should be harshly enforced, especially when black people are the ones who are guilty of the crime.

This abominable way of thinking extends to the continued Republican opposition to the use of other drugs, as well. The opioid crisis has disproportionately affected economically disadvantaged areas, regardless of race. The meth epidemic has followed a similar trajectory. As if Republicans' disastrous economic policies were not enough, they have to make sure to add insult to injury. Deregulation and corporate favoritism contributed to the worst recession we've seen since the Great Depression. As a result, people who have lost their jobs have to find a way to cope with the intense pain and anguish that economic instability brings. While there are better ways to do these things, unfortunately many of them turn to hard drug use. But even at that turn, they look down the barrel of lengthy prison sentences, all thanks to your friendly neighborhood Republican.

This is the clearest example of the need for Republicans to change course for the welfare of the American people. Drug use is entirely contained to the individual, and imprisoning drug users increases the Republicans' dreaded tax burden. But just when you thought that lowering taxes was the Republican golden goose, you find out that screwing over poor people and minorities means much more to them. Generally, they are far more transparent about their aims than they are with this policy. It takes some deciphering in order to discern what their true aim is. But now that we know, it is important to ensure that Republicans can no longer restrict the freedom of the American people in this manner. Vote your Republicans out of office and replace them with people who, at the very least, can respect your right to put whatever substance you want into your own body. You owe yourself that much.

6

INCOME INEQUALITY

Everyone receives benefits from society. When you live in a collective group, you generally give something to that group and receive something from the other members of that group. The balance of this give and take is what makes up the overall morale and economy of the group, and any aberrations are generally quickly remedied. This occurs either by force or by strong social coercion to achieve the aim that is best for the greatest number of people in the group. Humans have employed some variation of this paradigm in the vast majority of societies throughout history. There have been many exceptions, especially in strong dictatorships. But even in some dictatorships, life for most people is relatively equal, the dictator being the obvious exception.

America worked this way for most of its history. As prosperity increased, lawmakers recognized that it was important for the standard of living of the average person to increase in proportion to the level of wealth that the country as a whole controlled. As a result, we have a federal income tax to make people pay their fair share to bolster the society that helped to create them. The percentage of income increased in proportion to one's annual income in order to account for the fact that higher taxes harm rich people much less than they harm poor people. If you earn a million dollars a year, a fifty percent tax hurts you a lot less than it would hurt someone who earns twenty thousand dollars per year. At the end of the day, you'll still have five hundred thousand dollars per year.

This country has been able to support infrastructure projects and internal entitlement programs throughout the majority of the twentieth century in large part due to this tax structure. As people earned more money, the country took in more tax revenues. America began to enjoy one of the highest standards of living in the modern world. People started to depend on Social Security to provide them a stable income in retirement, the poor received healthcare, and food stamp programs ensured that we would not have hordes of people starving on the streets whenever a recession hit.

But then the Republicans took over, and they brought with them some of the most scathing tax reform policies the country had ever seen. Before you knew it, the top marginal tax rate in the federal income taxation scheme decreased precipitously, resulting in the comically low taxes on the rich we see today. Meanwhile, Republican administrations rallied to cut social entitlement programs in order to compensate for the decrease in government revenues. Republicans, as usual, explicitly favored the welfare of the rich at the expense of the welfare of the poor.

All of this would be palatable if Republicans did not continue to clamor for further tax cuts. Every time you see a Republican platform, proposed tax cuts feature prominently. The Trump administration passed a bill reducing taxes, primarily for the wealthy, and made it a heavy priority during its early days. This all comes in the face of a mounting national debt that requires tax revenues to contain. Republicans are always the first to call for a reduction in the national debt. They just want to eliminate the only way we have to pay off that debt. It's almost like they want to have their cake and eat it, too.

While Republicans call for a decrease in income taxes, the American people continue to suffer at the hands of a system that has more than enough to provide for the whole country but refuses to do so. If we have enough to go around while making sure that rich people still get to be rich, why do Republicans insist on decreasing taxes on those who are in the best position to help us prosper as a country? The answer is simple: Republicans only care about rich people. Most of them are rich people. It's in their best interest to care about helping the rich at the expense of the poor. The sooner we wake up and face this cold reality, the sooner we can push the oppressive rich minority off their perch of power.

You have to give Republicans credit for making a heck of a sales pitch, though. They are the first to parrot the "personal responsibility and hard work" school of how to move up the social ladder. But they refuse to acknowledge the reality that the vast majority of them came from places of extreme advantage that helped to keep them where they are. It's an unparalleled shell game. Working hard is great. Taking responsibility for your circumstances is admirable and ideal. But that's not enough for most people in the middle and lower classes to ascend the social hierarchy. If you think it is, you're living in a fantasy world.

It all comes from greed in its worst possible form. Republicans are more than happy to sit back and let poor people eat substandard food, live in substandard housing, and send their kids to substandard schools, all so that they can make sure they have enough money for their next yacht. We certainly shouldn't make rich people give up all their money for the common good. There has to be some room for ambition. But our current system is pathetic, and every attempt at "tax reform" somehow seems to make the rich richer and the poor poorer. It's funny how that always seems to happen during Republican administrations, isn't it?

Conservatives always respond that they are happy to give to charities in order to help make the world a better place, but that they don't want to be made to give money to an inefficient government. The problem with that line of reasoning is that we are all forced to pay money to the government in order to improve our country and provide for the less fortunate. Also, we know that conservatives aren't going to give the kind of money that is needed to keep people from starving in the streets, because they don't care about poor people. We can't forget that point. Republicans, and conservatives generally, could not care less about the fate of poor people, especially poor people of color.

We live as a collective society, despite the strength and vigor with which Republicans advocate for the liberty and potential of the individual. Americans drive on publicly funded roads, attend publicly funded schools, and depend on a publicly funded military for our national security. But Republicans act as though they do not benefit from these systems in the same way that we all do. Roads lead to rich people's businesses and carry their goods to the consumer. Their kids may not go to public schools, but almost everyone who works for them has children in public schools. Our military defends and upholds the constitution so that rich people can engage in free enterprise.

Rich people and Republicans benefit from collective resources, but they are trying to weasel their way out of paying their fair share of taxes to fund those resources. Some of them even have the gall to suggest that Congress should institute a so-called "flat tax" in order to solve the dilemma of taxation reform. The fact that Republicans suggest something should automatically set off alarm bells in your head. Republican policies almost universally favor rich, white, straight men or oppress everyone else. Their ideal platform does both, and the flat tax happens to be a Republican fantasy.

Picture the implementation of a flat tax and explain with a straight face how it does not explicitly favor the rich. Paying one's fair share is not about paying the exact same percentage of one's income as everyone else is required to. It's about paying the amount that one can afford to pay into the system while still retaining one's previous social status. If you institute a flat twenty-five percent tax, a poor person may be forced to pay as much as two or three times the amount that they were previously forced to pay. Meanwhile, a given rich person will get a tax cut that could be worth hundreds or thousands or millions of dollars depending on the person's circumstances. In what world is that fair? Again, the rich benefit and the poor suffer, just like Republicans have always wanted.

Assume that such a wretched tax plan were actually implemented. Someone who makes ten thousand dollars per year will be forced to pay twenty-five hundred dollars per year in taxes. That leaves them with only seventy-five hundred dollars to live on for an entire year. Someone who earns a million dollars a year will still get to have seven hundred fifty thousand dollars at the end of the year, which is far more than they would keep under the current system. The rich get richer and the poor get poorer. What else could you expect from a conservative platform?

What this country really needs is a massive redistribution of wealth in the form of increased taxation on the rich and increased social programs designed to assist the less fortunate. This is the only way that we can truly ensure social mobility while allowing people to keep just enough to make hard work desirable. Poor kids deserve a fair chance to succeed in this world, and the only way they can do that is to ensure that they can live in warm homes, eat good food, and go to good schools. Right now, they don't have access to any of those resources. Rich people have the absolute overabundance of money to make those dreams come true, but they horde their money and invest it to create more money. This money sits, trapped in the greedy paws of multi-billionaires rather than circulating in the economy where it belongs. What kind of system is that?

If you tax the rich, they'll still be rich, and we won't be on our way back to an age where rich people looked down on poor people starving to death in the streets. As it stands now, income inequality threatens to eat this country whole. Chances are, if you're reading this, you are directly affected by Republican greed and oppression. They sit in Washington and pass tax bill after tax bill designed to ensure that only you pay your fair share. Rich people make off like bandits and pass on increased profits to their shareholders. Meanwhile, you can't even afford to buy any stock and you stand one major medical crisis away from bankruptcy. You can barely tread water in the sea of student loan debt while the rich person plans their fourth, fifth, and sixth vacations of the year. You work for these people, and they actively plan to keep you from succeeding. They vote for Republicans who want to do the same.

You may not have the money necessary to fight back. It's okay. Most of us don't. But you do have a vote. Even in our corrupt system, you have the ability to raise your voice and say that you will not stand for continuing oppression. The only saving grace of income inequality is that it puts the majority of people in a similar situation. We are all being harmed by the greed of rich people, and those rich people are being bolstered by Republican policies and platforms. Together, we can stop this continued systematic assault from gaining steam and crushing all of us in the name of increased corporate profits and share prices. The law is here for a reason, and the law is only possible through the will of the people.

We are those people. The vast majority of us stand directly opposed to those forces being exerted upon us, and yet we remain complicit. Stand up and fight back against your captors. Do not succumb to economic Stockholm syndrome. Just because the rich employ you does not mean that you depend on them for value. Your value exists independent of a salary or a promotion. Our collective beauty radiates from our core and shines light on the plots and conspiracies that are formed in the dark hallways of mansions and in backrooms of Republican party gatherings.

We know where our bread is buttered, and we know that we can buy that butter from a different store. It's time to tell them that they can't control us, that we can think for ourselves, and that we can have everyone pay their fair share for resources that we all use. We can't afford to do anything else. Our health, happiness, and well-being all depend on us changing the course of history, and there's no better time to start than now.

7

GUNS

The death of a child is enough to tug at anyone's heartstrings. We are evolutionarily hard-wired to cringe at the mere idea that a child is being harmed. We know that it is in our collective best interest to ensure the health and well-being of future generations. That is, of course, unless you are a Republican.

It seems as though we are hearing about a new mass shooting every day, usually taking place in a school or at a large social gathering. These shootings often involve children, and sadly often result in the gruesome murder of large numbers of students. For most people with a heart, the answer to this solution is somewhat obvious. You find the source of the harm and you seek to minimize it without harming others in the process. For the gun control debate, that means banning the mass private ownership of guns, save for certain circumstances.

The debate intensifies as each new death toll scrolls across the news ticker. Parents cry for gun control as they mourn their deceased children, and Republicans turn a blind eye each and every time. They refuse to give up any ground and they cling to their assault weapons with an icy cold grip reminiscent of the Grim Reaper himself. This problem has a solution, and those who stand on the Republican side of the aisle actively oppose any measure that could help to protect the lives of American schoolchildren. I stop just short of saying that they actually want these children to be shot, but they're doing just as much harm through their ignorance.

Make no mistake, Republicans, the blood of the men, women, and children who have died in mass shootings in the twenty-first century is all on your hands. You had the opportunity to admit that the Second Amendment is a relic of the era of redcoats and revolutionaries, and that it no longer has a place in American society. Don't act as though you need a weapon to overcome the tyrannical government that you continue to prattle on about in your tin-hat conspiracy sessions. Even if the government became tyrannical, none of you have the weaponry necessary to overcome the might of the United States military. Your shotgun or pistol can't do anything against a tank. If they want you, they're going to come get you, and there's nothing you can do about it.

Every time there's a school shooting, you see some right-wing parent come out and say that they are no longer in favor of the mass arming of the American citizenry. These brave men and women have put their country over their party and admitted that we have a serious problem. Some of them have even given up their guns and conceded that it is better for a child to go to school without fear of being shot than it is for them to own a gun that gathers dust in their safe. We need these people on our side, and I believe the numbers are growing each and every day.

If the prevalence of guns in this country has led to an increase in mass shootings and other gun-related fatalities, and I believe it has, then why do Republicans continue to push a pro-Second Amendment platform? You've been reading this book long enough to know the answer. They're selfish people. They don't care about dead children as long as they can keep their precious guns. Republicans fantasize about situations in which they will need to "protect themselves" from intruders and shoot the perpetrator dead on the front porch. It's almost perverse.

But these people live in some of the safest areas of the country.

They largely live in suburbs that have robust police forces that are more than capable of enforcing the rule of law. Their arguments are the delusions of a people who continually feel the need to paint themselves as victims of some sort of mythical oppression. It's no coincidence that the vast majority of gun rights advocates are white male Republicans. These are people who feel that their country is being taken away from them, particularly through the advancement of civil rights and the increased success of minorities in America.

Having access to weapons girds them against what they perceive to be the real threats facing them in twenty-first century America. It's their last bastion of hope in the face of overwhelming societal progress that threatens to leave them behind. Since the Republican party is the party of rich, white, straight men, it should come as no surprise that Republicans want to keep these people armed. They think a war is coming, and they want to make sure that white men are prepared.

Think about it. Republicans don't really care about advocating for the right of all Americans to keep and bear arms. The right-wing establishment advocates for stronger policing, and strong police forces continually prosecute minorities for carrying weapons. But whenever a black person gets arrested for carrying a gun, it's fine because the "gun wasn't registered". So clearly the person intended to commit a crime with it. However, when white people are arrested for carrying unregistered arms, all of a sudden gun policy is too restrictive and needs to be loosened in order to accommodate the rights of the American people. You truly cannot win with these people.

It is important that you take this issue as personally as possible. There is no room for disagreement on this issue. To the extent that you know someone who opposes gun control, remember that you know someone who will turn a blind eye if your child is killed in a school shooting. This is what Republicans stand for. They want white men to be able to clutch their toys of death, no matter how many children have to die in the process. It's truly evil.

If you engage in an argument with a Republican regarding gun control, you'll likely hear them talk about the need to uphold the Second Amendment. If you hang around long enough, you'll hear a discussion of the intention of the founding fathers and about how they truly intended for the American people to be armed in order to defend against a tyrannical government. It's important to realize two points. First of all, the intent of the founding fathers is irrelevant when children are dying from gunshot wounds inflicted by weapons that the founding fathers could never have dreamed of. Second, the constitution is meant to be a living document. If our interpretation of the law cannot change as the needs of the people change, then the system as a whole is incredibly flawed.

Republicans hardly care about the constitution when it comes to their desire to regulate how other people conduct themselves. (See, again, the abortion debate generally.) Don't believe them for one second when they pay lip service to constitutional originalism. They only care about it when it suits their needs. This is purely about their refusal to give up anything in order to serve the greater good. If they like it, they're not giving it up, no matter how many people it can help. They like money, so they advocate against taxes. They like guns, so they refuse to give up guns. The only time they want to get rid of something is if it benefits the rest of us. They do not have the collective interest of the American people at heart, as is easily demonstrated by their upturned noses at each and every story of children killed in school shootings.

We can't give one inch in this debate. Lives are literally on the line, and there is a great deal of money and influence standing in our way. I don't want to get rid of every gun in the country. That's not feasible policy, and it's not fair to those who want to use guns for sport and for hunting. But I do want to make it incredibly difficult for someone to get their hands on a gun. They should have to go through extensive background checks, be subject to mental health screenings, demonstrate that they have knowledge of gun safety, and show that they have an actual need to own a gun. These should be the minimum requirements to qualify for gun ownership in the United States. This keeps guns out of the hands of certain dangerous individuals while ensuring that those who qualify have the ability to purchase a gun.

This issue is not difficult. I readily admit that many disagreements between people on the left and people on the right are due to legitimate differences in worldview, and that debates should be had in order to enhance our understanding. But there's no room for debate here. Children are dying and Republicans refuse to enact measures that can keep that from happening. This is all, of course, so that they can hold on to their precious guns as they claim the founding fathers intended. This is vanity at the expense of the lives of innocent human beings. The fact that these mass shootings still happen is proof that our current policy is not working, and Republicans are to blame for the obstacles standing between us and sensible gun reform.

Just as they have no mercy on children who simply want to attend school without fear of being shot, we should have no mercy on Republicans at the polls. Vote all of them out, one by one, until they realize that the American people will not agree to live in a country where guns flood the streets and fear permeates our schools. Our collective conscience can and should change policy on this issue. We can do better than this, and we have to do better than this. If the lives of innocent men, women, and children matter less than the right of people to own guns that are used to take those lives, how can we claim any moral superiority as a country? Republicans do not care about morals or the value of human life, despite their stance on abortion (which I will discuss later). Every time you go to the polls, make sure you impose the will of the American people upon their immoral and abominable ideology. Until real gun reform comes, we cannot afford to be silent.

8

ABORTION

The right of American women to secure access to abortion services has long been a point of contention in American political discourse. Many people have legitimate disagreements with legalized abortion due to their belief that life begins at conception. For some people, this comes from their views on moral philosophy. For most others, it comes from a prescribed dogma laid out in various religious traditions. In any event, Republicans have taken up the so-called "pro-life" cause and made it one of their defining stances. Their vociferous opposition to abortion has resulted in some of the most vitriolic dialogue concerning a political issue in American history.

It's important to look at the set of opinions here before casting judgement, which I will admit I fully intend to do. The liberal position, generally referred to as the "pro-choice" stance, contends that a woman should be free to make whatever choices she wants to make with her body in and of itself. To pro-choice people, any infringement by the government on a woman's right to choose what she does with her own body is a grave overstep and an unjust restriction on personal liberty. This includes limiting the right to procure an abortion

The conservative and Republican stance, generally referred to as the "pro-life" stance, argues that a fetus is a person with all the attendant rights and moral standing. The argument then follows that a woman's right to choose stops when it affects the life or well-being of the fetus, and therefore killing a fetus should be illegal. Most pro-life individuals consider life to begin at conception, and that any and all abortion should be proscribed by law.

The Republican stance on this issue is morally and sociologically idiotic. If life begins at conception, then Republicans want us to believe that a clump of cells has the same moral personhood as a fully-grown adult. You can see why this makes absolutely no sense. The fact that something has the potential to become something does not mean that it deserves to be treated as if it is the thing it may become. When I say "may", I mean to say that there is no guarantee that a fetus will end up becoming a baby, no matter how hard we wish it to be so.

This point matters because potentiality cannot serve as a proxy for moral protection. With modern technology, many things can turn into several other things, and Republicans have conveniently drawn the line in the sand at the point of conception. Should it be immoral for a man to masturbate, since his sperm could become a fetus when combined with an egg. Is menstruation morally problematic even though it is not intentional? Why do we draw the line at fetuses?

Further, a fetus is nothing more than a likely future person. Does a fetus that is virtually guaranteed to be stillborn still have the rights of a person before it dies? It does not have the potential to become a person, but it still has a heartbeat in its mothers womb. There are several genetic conditions that result in stillbirth being far more likely than live birth. To Republicans, it is immoral to abort such a fetus, and they believe it should be illegal. They would rather put a woman through the immense pain and trauma of carrying a fetus to stillbirth than allow her to end the process, grieve, and move on with her life. What kind of people would legally foist such suffering on a woman in that position?

The answer is quite simple. Republicans do not care about the health and welfare of women. They have demonstrated that they care about the lives of mere clusters of cells more than they care about the lives of fully formed adult women. Pregnancy carries many inherent and obvious health risks, and yet Republicans would legally force women to endure these risks just to save a fetus. What sense does that make? Some Republicans have come to their senses and admitted that abortion should be legal in cases where the mother's life is at risk. However, they have a very narrow interpretation of what that risk is. They generally believe that an abortion should be legal unless the mother is in active distress and is at risk of dying in the near future. Intense pain and illness, short of imminent death, is apparently not enough for Republicans to admit that abortion should be an option. What an embarrassing point of view.

Republicans claim to be the party of individual liberty and small government. But apparently they believe government should be exactly the size of the average woman's uterus, because that is precisely the space that Republicans want policy to occupy. They want to be free from paying taxes to support common resources, but the ability to remove something from one's own body is apparently too much liberty for them to handle. I know this is a recurring theme in this book, but Republicans only care about themselves. They advocate for personal liberty when it suits their needs, but they are the first ones to stand against the right of a person to choose what they do with their own body whenever it doesn't fit the Republican cause.

Again, Republicans stand against abortion rights because those who have the most to lose in this battle are not people that Republicans actually care about. You'll remember from earlier chapters that Republicans really only care about the lives and welfare of rich, straight, white men of means. That's it. If you don't fall within that narrow demographic, don't expect the Republicans to care if you live or die, let alone have the ability to choose what to do with your own body. They'll always favor guns over social programs, criminalizing drugs over people enjoying a joint, and their own religion over a woman's right to choose. These are truly selfish individuals who have no business forming policy that affects people outside of their bigoted, oppressive bubble.

The average Republican has no idea what women go through, and they have no clue of the cost that carrying a pregnancy to term imposes on the average women. Between income inequality and a lack of privilege, many women in this country are not suitably financially equipped to comfortably handle an unexpected pregnancy. The hospital bills alone are more than most people in this situation would be able to absorb. That, of course, doesn't include the costs of food, clothing, shelter, and healthcare for the little one. All of these costs are forced upon women by oppressive Republican regimes that don't have to bear them. Remember, this is the party of straight, white, rich men. These men don't get pregnant, and therefore have no idea what women go through in society. Maybe they should be made to live one day in the life of the average American woman. Maybe then they would change their tune.

The real reason that Republicans want to enact draconian legislation banning abortion is because it is an issue that involves women and their genitals. These men are not comfortable with women having agency over their own bodies, and abortion is arguably one of the strongest expressions of agency. It is the ability to say that a given set of circumstances will not determine how one lives one's life. Republicans don't want women to have any power. It's why they don't run women for the presidency. If they can force a woman to do something, or keep a woman from doing something that benefits her, they're going to take that opportunity every time without fail. These are sexist, bigoted, privileged individuals who use their power to try to keep women down.

One of the purest examples of this comes in the existence of Republicans who would ban abortion even when a woman is raped or is the victim of incest. Besides allowing abortion to save the life of the mother, these two instances would appear to most sane people as the most sensible exceptions to any proposed abortion regulation. But many Republicans don't even want to allow this. To them, the good lord in heaven has a reason for everything, and foisting the results of sexual assault on a rape survivor is the only way that the divine will can truly be expressed. What a sick and twisted god they have concocted in their heads. Don't be fooled by their country boy hucksterism. They want to stick rape survivors with the non-consensual products of their assault, and make the elimination of those products illegal. I'm sure many of these awful people believe that these rape survivors somehow deserved it. But we'll get to more specific issues of women's rights in a later chapter.

These men have not been the victims of sexual assault. For them to even pretend to understand the psyche of a survivor is the height of political injury. To make these survivors carry the perpetrator's fetus to term just adds insult to that injury. These people do not care about women. Republican lawmakers ostensibly have mothers, daughters, sisters, and aunts. Do these women know that their sons, fathers, brothers, and nephews are actively working to undercut their rights, one by one? They must rationalize it somehow. Otherwise, they would be marching in the streets, telling anyone who would listen that their relative is a spineless piece of human garbage who seeks to undercut their very existence at every turn.

Keep in mind that many of these Republican lawmakers have wives. These brutal, heartless, oppressive men somehow conned these poor women into agreeing to be their wives. Worse yet, these women likely agreed to have sex with these miserable wretches. I can't imagine the level of persuasiveness that an average Republican congressman has to possess in order to successfully woo a romantic partner. Maybe that's why they're congressmen. They are apparently very successful at pulling the wool over the eyes of the people they claim to care about. Women, if you have any sense, you'll withhold sex from these men until they agree to place your personhood above the so-called "rights" of a small set of cells. Maybe then you'll also discover that they care more about their sex drive than they do about their beloved principles. When you lack a real moral compass, it's easy to move from priority to priority with ease, ignoring your own hypocrisy along the way.

That's what Republicans really are, at their core. They're scummy, hypocritical dirtbags who only care about their own lives and welfare. Corporations have similar rights to people, and newly formed zygotes have a right to life, but a woman can't even do what she wants with her own body. This is more than a case of misplaced priorities. This is active hatred of women. Republicans despise the idea of women having control over anything involving their own bodies, especially their genitals. If anyone tried to restrict the right of men to masturbate the way that Republicans want to restrict the right of a woman to obtain an abortion, the government would be overthrown tomorrow. The force would be overwhelming and the response would be swift.

This is an issue you can fight back on. We vote for lawmakers. We vote for presidents. Presidents appoint Supreme Court justices who dictate the law on this issue from the lofty heights of the bench. We possess a voice, but that voice is waning amidst the din of precedent and decades of policy eroding the right of a woman to choose. Perhaps the only thing more important than our collective voice at the polls is the influence of the women in the lives of these despicable men. Military conflicts have been started and ended by great women. Sex strikes have moved more men to true compassion than the threat of eternal damnation. This time, the assault is on your rights, ladies. Your loved one stands for policy that tells you that you can't choose. Just as men stood against women's suffrage, they continue to stand against female choice. They view it as a threat to men. If they didn't, they wouldn't really have a reason to care.

Republicans have put this issue in the most disgusting of terms. They refuse to use the term "fetus", instead strongly preferring the term "baby", even for freshly-formed zygotes. Conservatives have turned this into an issue of baby killers versus those heroic crusaders who actively campaign to save their lives from the evil, awful women who carry them <u>as part of their own bodies</u>. Never mind the fact that they conveniently refuse to characterize the gun control debate this way, when actual children are actually dying at the hands of people holding guns that should have been banned long ago. You can smell the hypocrisy from miles away.

Republicans don't care about children any more than they care about women, minorities, or anyone other than rich, white, straight men. Selfishness and greed follow them like a storm cloud, dumping an acrid rain on their lives and the lives of anyone unfortunate enough to care about them. Don't give them the benefit of the doubt. They'd sooner sell women as a whole down the river for another tax break. That has been proven every time a Republican lawmaker stands up and argues against abortion rights while children continue to starve in every American city. Do they care about children or not? The answer should be abundantly clear.

9
______

DEATH PENALTY

The criminal justice system lends itself well toward the unique forms of cruelty and oppression that Republicans have used to make their mark on the world. If you actively seek to oppress people, and Republicans always seek to do that through their policies, then wielding the powerful sword of imprisonment and punishment goes further than any restrictions on otherwise free people could.

No source of criminal punishment is more powerful than that of the death penalty. Despite the fact that it has been abolished in many developed and civilized countries, Republicans have succeeded in ensuring that the death penalty persists in some form in many American states and at the federal level. It has become a uniquely conservative cause and, fittingly, has served as a sign that our country is behind the times in so many crucial ways. The sheer barbarism of killing people as a penalty for committing a crime cannot be understated. It's no great shock that Republicans continue to advocate for it.

The scope of offenses that qualify for the death penalty have largely narrowed as our country has progressed socially. Now, the death penalty is only permissible as a result of conviction for a handful of crimes. Even though the use of capital punishment is dwindling in other countries, Republicans insist on holding firm to a commitment of killing people for committing crimes. What else is new?

It's important to look at why the Republican stance on the death penalty is uniquely and savagely hypocritical. To being with, the death penalty is a joke of a punishment for those who have committed the most heinous of crimes. Even if we set aside the fact that the criminal justice system is supposed to be about rehabilitation rather than punishment, the death penalty does not inspire the fear that other, worse fates do. Republicans will never believe in prison as being rehabilitative, because they value inflicting pain on others over actual justice. But death is hardly the worst fate that one can experience, as countless experience and allegories have collectively taught us as a society.

Imagine that someone presented you with two options after you have been convicted of first-degree murder. The first option is life in prison without the possibility of parole. The second option is the death penalty. Is there any question that the second option is better than the first? We all have an instinctive fear of death, but death is certainly better than a life of certain pain and seemingly never-ending misery. Prisons in this country are in a laughably atrocious state, and many of us would not wish life imprisonment on even our worst enemies. Rampant sexual assault, disease, and violence comprise the realities of life for many people in high security prisons. Forcing someone to live out their remaining days in these conditions is far more of a punishment than sticking a needle in their arm and stopping their heart.

If this is the case, then why do Republicans insist on advocating for the death penalty over life imprisonment? Again, Republicans are driven by a bloodthirsty desire for vengeance and an overwhelming attraction to anything that acts in their best interests. To Republicans, the death penalty is appropriate because it hearkens back to a time when the rule of "an eye for an eye" won the day. This was a far simpler time, when complex and extensive systems of government and criminal justice had not yet been discovered. Such a lack of civility is an unfortunate heirloom of our ill-formed past as a species. That said, those are clearly the times to which Republicans long to return.

The death penalty works to the advantage of Republicans for several reasons. First, it is undeniable that the death penalty disproportionately affects black people. This sad state of affairs marries the two halves of the Republican doublethink, a proclaimed reverence for human life and a disdain for the value of black lives, perfectly in the greater milieu of political discourse in this country. It's the best way that one can pay lip service to the value of human life while celebrating the end of black lives. After all, these Republicans only claim to want to see justice done. They want the parents of children who have been murdered to watch the warden read the death warrant of the man who took their child away from them. Even to the most evolved and progressive among us, there is something viscerally satisfying about this sort of "justice".

But this is a situation in which Republicans are, at best, lying to themselves. You cannot claim to cherish life, particularly black lives, and say that the death penalty is a good thing for society. No matter how much you want to pettifog the issue, the two concepts are mutually exclusive. But Republicans don't actually care about life. Anyone can see that after talking to a Republican about gun control. Also, it should be blatantly clear that Republican's could not care less about the legitimacy and welfare of black lives. We've seen that in their reaction to the start of the Black Lives Matter movement. Instead, they just want to exact revenge for the sake of exacting revenge. Barbaric behavior not only has a place in American society, according to Republicans, but it deserves a spot on our proverbial pedestal right next to guns and walls built to keep out immigrants.

If Republicans really cared about the value of life, they would admit that courts and juries have been wrong regarding murder convictions in the past. Numerous legal projects exist around the country to ensure that those who have been wrongfully convicted can one day be exonerated and released from prison. Many successful clients of these programs have been on death row. If we can admit that convictions are often wrong, then we should be able to admit that an irreversible penalty is not an appropriate punishment for these offenses. Even though imprisonment is unjustifiable in the case of an innocent person, at least someone can be released from prison if they are later found to be innocent. They can also receive financial compensation for their pain and suffering. Death does not enjoy such luxuries.

But Republicans favor the quick and easy solution. They would rather just rid themselves of the convicted person, without any further inquiry into their potential innocence. It is a disgusting position, one that reveals the truly vile underbelly of their philosophy. Some of them would counter by saying that certain individuals are too dangerous to be allowed to live. They might cite noted organized crime leaders, who can often direct criminal activities from within prison walls. When these people are convicted for capital offenses, the argument goes, the world remains unsafe even if they are incarcerated in maximum-security facilities. As a result, the death penalty is the only way to ensure that society can be safe from the evils of these criminals.

That's a nice line of thought if you forget about how America's prison systems actually work. Most maximum-security facilities make it nigh impossible for criminals to conduct the sorts of activities that this argument contemplates. Even if Republicans are worried about the security of these facilities, surely they must know about the existence of supermax facilities. These prisons house the most dangerous criminals the world has ever seen, and they cannot conduct criminal activities from behind those doors. If Republicans truly cared about the value of human life, they would certainly prefer to keep someone alive in one of these institutions rather than sentencing them to death.

But that's just the problem. Republicans don't care about the inherent worth of human life if it doesn't involve regulating a woman's genitals. If it only involves a convicted felon's right to life, all of a sudden human life doesn't mean quite as much. It's the height of hypocrisy, but no one will hold them accountable on the issue. Either human life matters or it doesn't. Republicans can't have it both ways, yet American voters continue to let them have their cake and eat it too, every time they go to the polls. Hypocrisy is shameful enough in and of itself. But when that hypocrisy involves the way that one values human life, then priorities are clearly out of place. This should come as no surprise when it comes to the stances of the Republican party.

The real reason that Republicans fetishize the death penalty is that it's another way that they can take rights away from someone else. They value life in the context of the abortion debate because restricting abortion takes rights away from pregnant women. But when they have the opportunity to stand up and defend convicts' right to life, they refuse to do so because they see another set of rights that can be taken away. Surely, the mere argument that human beings have inherent worth and a right to live cannot overcome the tantalizing possibility of stripping rights from another human being.

This is especially true when the person losing their right to life is a person of color. Since convicts are generally disproportionately people of color due to the flaws in our criminal justice system, advocating for the death penalty is akin to advocating for the end of black lives. When you cast the issue this way, it really comes as no surprise that Republicans so love capital punishment. They'd probably seek to expand it if they could.

10

WOMEN'S RIGHTS

Courageous pioneers have been fighting for the rights of women in this country for centuries. Basic necessities such as the right to vote, the right to enjoy one's own property, and the right to not be the property of another were once risky and fundamental struggles for women. Luckily, most of society has increasingly recognized that women and men should have equal rights. But a select group of people want to send America back to the wild west with respect to women's rights. They are almost all ardent Republicans.

A running theme throughout this book has been that Republicans are interested in nothing more than preserving the rights and liberties of rich, straight, white men at the expense of minorities and women. Republican stances on women's issues should hardly be a shock to the prudent observer, then. They seek to hamper the potential for women to advance and potentially overtake the rich, white men who have been favored in America for most of our country's history. Keep in mind, Republicans are generally rich, white men, so they are arguably acting in their own self-interest.

However, subjugating the rights of another so that you can thrive is an exercise in true evil, and Republicans have whipped themselves into impeccable shape. It comes naturally to them now. Perhaps it always did. Even apart from the abortion debate, as is discussed elsewhere in this book, Republicans have stood in the way of strong and powerful women at every turn. The party doesn't even run women for the presidency. Some of the most prominent Republicans are women, but the party thinks so little of them that I doubt they have ever even thought of putting a woman first on the ballot. The perceived threat to the superiority of white men is so powerful, that they arguably have put the future of their own party in jeopardy by refusing to consider presidential candidates based on the genitals of the person in question. It's truly abhorrent.

The disdain that Republicans have for women knows no bounds. They don't argue in favor of positions that women have identified as being truly beneficial for gender equality. The hatred starts with their decidedly strong opinion against birth control and the free distribution of contraceptives. For a party that claims to value personal liberty and the ability to control one's body, the Republican party sure has a funny way of showing appreciation for the ability of women to control their own procreative actions. Even when this country had the closest thing it has ever had to universal healthcare, Republicans pushed and rallied for the right of employers to refuse to cover contraceptive medication under their employee healthcare plans.

I truly believe that Republicans could not care less about the rights of small business owners to express their religious beliefs. The answer is much simpler than that. Republicans truly view women as vessels for the reproductive whims of men. To a Republican, women should have no agency of their own, as they are inherently inferior to men. Their only value is to be barefoot and pregnant in the kitchen, subservient to the desires of their oppressive husbands. If a woman somehow rejects the idea of being a mother at any time, that is an affront in the eyes of conservatives. To do so is to somehow shun the true purpose and nature of what it means to be a woman. It's interesting that Republicans have such strongly-held beliefs on this issue, considering that so many of them are men. But when you believe that men are superior to women in every way, it makes sense to think that men know more about what it means to be a woman than women do. It is pure, unbridled arrogance.

To Republicans, a woman who desires to take contraceptive medication is a hussy, a whore, or a degenerate. To freely desire sex and wish to control its consequences flies in the face of whatever Republicans believe that the divine plan is for women. In their eyes, men are to dictate women's sexuality, and any deviation from that norm is to be despised and shamed. That's why some conservatives are in favor of prescribing contraceptive medication to married couples. If a married couple requests the pill, then the man likely had a say in making that decision. This male input validates the choice to prevent pregnancy. But male sexuality is not to be restricted at all. Male virility and sex drive are the highest prize in American society, and every measure will be taken to ensure that it reaches its natural goal if Republicans have anything to say about it. That's why you don't hear Republicans rallying against erectile dysfunction medication. So many of them have to use it that it would work against their interests to speak out against its use.

Republicans are so heartless that they don't even care about the unintended side effects of their anti-contraception stance. They haven't done enough research or learned enough biology to understand that hormonal contraception has multiple uses. It is not only used to prevent pregnancy. It can be used to control disastrous symptoms of menstruation in certain women, and can also be used to correct hormonal imbalances. In certain cases, it is also used to chemically castrate convicted sex offenders. Something tells me that Republicans would actually favor this use, since it can actively take something away from someone else and punish them for a crime. Chemically castrating pedophiles might be the only thing that I agree with Republicans about.

That being said, I'm sure that Republicans are privately in favor of using contraception when it suits their own interests. I'm sure scores of Republican lawmakers wear condoms when they're having sex with their mistresses or insist that those same mistresses take the pill in order to avoid an unexpected pregnancy. See, the upside of having no true moral compass is that one is never really forced to face up to hypocrisy. If your only principle is selfishness, you only have to care about those things that affect you. This is all somewhat rational from the Republican viewpoint, because they don't care about anyone other than themselves. When you combine that self-centeredness with the power that Republicans have been able to accrue over the years, the result is unchecked danger for anyone outside the fold.

But just to show that they stand against women at literally every stage in their lives, from conception until natural death and possibly even beyond in the case of religious people, conservatives continue to advocate against laws mandating employers to provide maternity leave for their female employees. Most of these men have never had to take primary responsibility for child care, so why would they ever admit that it requires some time off in order to do correctly? Conveniently, they cite the need to provide employers with the liberty to make employment decisions for themselves and not to have those decisions be conditioned on federal law. It's amazing how Republicans duck and dodge personal liberty when they want to, isn't it? Motherhood is incredibly difficult, and any mother who is reading this knows that it takes time to acclimate to life with a child. Just keeping a kid alive is incredibly difficult work. Women deserve the time off to make sure that their child has the best possible start in life. After all, at least when it comes to wives of Republicans, we can be sure that their husbands aren't going to do it for them.

Republicans have always been committed to the image of the typical family. But this is likely due to the fact that the American archetype of the nuclear family prizes the position of the male as the head of the household and breadwinner. Meanwhile, the woman of the house is relegated to a second-class background role as mother and primary operator of the household. When you have all the glory, it's easy to oppress the person you have already relegated to the silver medal. Men are not expected to raise children, so they should really have no say in whether employers should be required to provide maternity leave for their employees. They lack the necessary context necessary to weigh in on that issue. Until men have to push a baby out through their genitals, they need to stay out of the debate entirely and simply trust that women know what they're talking about. Cue the collective male cringe. It's beautiful.

Conservatives have largely rallied against the legalization of prostitution, in yet another grand ploy to deny women the agency to control their own sexual and reproductive decisions. Considering how many Republican lawmakers have been caught with prostitutes, you would think that they would have a vested interest in legalizing it. But denying women the right to control their own bodies means just that much to them. They won't give it up for anything, no matter how hard you try. When consensual prostitution occurs outside of the context of pimping and human trafficking, it literally has no victims so long as other laws against violent behavior are enforced. It cultivates and supports a free market, that pesky little thing that Republicans love to go on about preserving. Prostitution as a political issue is almost uniquely teed up for Republican support.

But, to them, vaginas are icky and gross, and the idea of a woman selling access to her own invokes that childlike image of cooties and shame that accompanied the girl who kissed one too many boys on the playground. To the extent that a woman uses her vagina for anything other than pleasing her husband or having a baby with her husband, Republicans oppose it. They will be the first to stand up and demand that a woman's use of her own genitals be regulated while saying the risky gambling that banks engage in with depositor money should not only be deregulated, but encouraged. What a sick state of affairs.

Not only do Republicans want to deny a woman the right to choose what she does with her own body, they fundamentally deny the gender pay gap. It has become incredibly obvious in modern American society that women are very often paid less than men for performing the same job. This is a societally acceptable relegation of woman to subhuman status. Ostensibly, if someone performs a job, they deserve the money that comes with that job because they provide skills and utility as a person and as a worker. By denying women their true value in the workplace, the gender pay gap denies the equal personhood of women. In refusing to admit that this is a problem, Republicans do the same thing. One of the most potent things that can be done to increase social equality is to advocate for the rights of women. Increasing the standing of women in the world starts with ensuring that they are compensated fairly for the work they do. But Republicans refuse to admit that there's even a problem here.

There's a very good reason why this issue is so salient in current political discourse. Any disagreement here has to do with the core tenet that women are equal to men and should be treated as such. To the extent that anyone disagrees with this or works against treating women the same way men are treated has a hand in shaping society so that it favors men. In doing this, they send a message to young women that they shouldn't even bother trying to succeed. Republicans have daughters, and they are clearly just fine with telling them that they are somehow less than their brothers. Silencing women starts at an incredibly young age, and Republicans may as well be elementary school teachers with the amount of influence they wield over young female minds. They should be ashamed of themselves and everything they stand for.

The entire Republican message is designed to oppress women and then tell them that all of their problems are their own fault. They run on a platform of personal liberty and responsibility, but their policies have resulted in a society where women have a disproportionately difficult time getting ahead. They socialize young women into thinking that they should only enter a select number of professions, most of which pay far less than the jobs that they tell young boys to aspire to. Then society expect women to exit that career path to get married and have children, shaming those who choose to remain career-oriented and driven. On top of all that, Republicans want to ensure that women never have a say over the operation and use of their own genitals. Can you imagine if the same conditions were applied to white men? There would be rioting and marching in the streets. But Republicans are uniquely adept at making life hard for women in the United States, so the streets remain empty.

The beautiful thing about the female demographic is that it represents the majority of the American population. Unlike racial and ethnic minorities, women really can band together and bring about substantial change that values their existence and legitimacy as people. The only question is: What's holding you back. Women, come together and express a unique voice at the polls. Tell Republicans that you won't stand for their nonsense anymore. Tell them you've had enough. Stand up for your genitals, and tell these white men to keep their grubby hands off. Tell them to stop grabbing you by the pussy, lest you turn around and grab them by the balls.

11

LGBT RIGHTS

The advance of LGBT rights in the United States could be accurately described as a proper and meteoric rise. From open homophobia being accepted less than a decade ago to same-sex marriage being legal and trans rights becoming more and more prominent on the progressive agenda, the outlook on the horizon is good. But we still have more work to do. The primary enemy of progress in the area of LGBT rights is not so much the lagging of society at this point, but the ardent hatred that Republicans have for LGBT people. This has been very clearly demonstrated, particularly within the last twenty-five years, and there is really no sign of it going away any time soon.

Being LGBT is inherently outside the norm, especially when LGBT identities are considered against the background of the majority of the American populace. But as countless demographics have taught us, the fact that there are fewer of us does not mean that we are any less special than members of majority groups. Granting basic rights to members of the LGBT community should be a priority for any legislative agenda, and Democrats have cherished these fights for a long time now. But Republicans still feel the need to take something away from people, so they actively stand in the way of any progress with respect to LGBT rights. Remember, Republicans only care about straight, rich, white men. If you lose any one of these characteristics, you are automatically considered to be out of the club and thus not worthy of their protection.

To start, Republicans have notably opposed legalizing same-sex marriage since the debate gained serious ground in the late twentieth and early twenty-first centuries. Luckily for society, they lost the fight and same-sex marriage is now legal nationwide (for now). But most Republicans remain steadfast in their position that marriage is only between one man and one woman. Their rationale for this is almost entirely religious. These people come from strong, Christian churches and believe that anyone who believes something different than what they believe is going to hell. There's nothing wrong with Christianity per se, but it has made people do some terrible things in society. We'll get to that later.

Fundamentally, Republicans misunderstand what the meaning of marriage is. That is why they think that a man and a woman who are only connected by an unplanned pregnancy have more business being married than two men who have loved each other for years. Marriage is about love. It is about loving someone so much that you cannot live without them. It is about willing to suffer when they suffer, laugh when they laugh, and cry when they cry. But Republicans just don't see that. To them, marriage is about gender and genitalia. If they don't "fit", then they don't belong together in the eyes of conservatives. Considering how many Republicans have had publicly disastrous affairs and divorces, one would think that they'd be willing to take a hint from gays and lesbians regarding the foundations of marriage.

Generally, as American society heard more stories and testimonials from LGBT individuals, our collective attitude began to soften. Parents listened to their children come out over dinner, painful stories regarding bullying and discrimination were shared, and prominent individuals openly identified as either LGBT or allies. A transformation of opinion occurred right before our eyes. We watched a new civil rights movement crop up, bloom, and flourish within little more than a decade. Ultimately, the struggle culminated in a Supreme Court decision legalizing marriage equality.

But Republicans stood in the way with every opportunity they got. From DOMA to individual states banning same-sex marriage through constitutional amendments, they tried to put up roadblock after roadblock all along the road to equality. The only reason they stopped talking about it so much is that the Supreme Court finally shut them up and left them with little recourse for achieving their aims. The same theme of Republican obstinacy runs through this debate, as well. An opportunity presented itself to deprive a group of happiness and fulfillment. The fact that this group was, by definition, not made up of straight, white men made their decision all the easier. All they have ever cared about is maintaining what they believe to be the American norm and American ideals. This means one man, one woman, a few kids, a dog, a picket fence, and a whole pile of money made from big businesses that actively antagonize the collective welfare of the American people. Anything that falls outside of this paradigm deserves to be beaten and broken, according to Republicans.

As we saw, the will of the masses does not take kindly to the political maneuvers that Republicans often employ in an attempt to get their way. The American people decided that Republicans were wrong, and moved remarkably quickly to undo all the harm that they managed to do with decades of legislation. America decided that gay people mattered and that their lives meant just as much as anyone else's. More and more people were recruited to the right side of history. Perhaps this would be better called the "left side of history". People went to the polls, voted out those politicians who sought to deny their sons and daughter the right to enjoy life with the person they love, and demanded that federal law recognize the rights they craved. As a result, we went from calling gay people vile names on primetime television to announcing marriage equality in the Supreme Court in around a decade.

When a critical debate ends, both sides usually retreat, with one celebrating victory and the other trying to handle defeat the best way it can. But generally the war ends and people try to return to the civility they had before the political storm. I don't think we can afford to do that here. Republicans did not suddenly become pro-gay when that decision was read from the highest bench in the land. They just resolved to go underground, where homophobia and gay-bashing fester and ferment. This fight is not over. Republicans are just recoiling. They will fight to put conservative justices on the Court who want to overturn marriage equality. We cannot forgive Republicans for the sins of their past if they do not make a genuine attempt to apologize and change their future. There is too much at stake, and mercy is not feasible. If we don't defend the rights we fought so hard for, we cannot expect anyone else to do it for us. The ground we gained will fall once more to Republicans if we do not stand and go to war to protect it.

In addition to readying ourselves to go back to war over marriage equality, we must take up a position to defend the trans community. Now that Republicans are licking their chops from the beating that SCOTUS handed them in the same-sex marriage case, they have turned their sights toward vilifying trans people. Again, these are straight, white, rich men attempting to beat and break anyone that is different from them. Trans individuals throw the very concept of gender into question. A firm idea of gender is all that is holding many of these frail people together. Their confidence is tied to their masculinity, and they will fight back against anything that threatens to redefine it. Republicans have already demonstrated that they will do anything in their power to keep trans people from being happy and enjoying their best lives.

They have stood in the way of allowing trans people to use restrooms that correspond to their gender identities. Of course, cis people are allowed to express their gender identities however they want in Republicanland. But conservative lawmakers insist on going on cable news networks to stir up fear in their base regarding trans people using a bathroom. They claim that their children are in danger because trans people are using the bathroom. Because a trans woman might have male genitalia, they believe their daughters are at risk somehow. They ignore the fact that we already have laws to prohibit any behavior that they fear. If someone harms a woman or a child in a women's restroom, that person can be charged with a litany of crimes under criminal statutes in every state. But Republicans have to add one more law to ensure that this specific community is targeted. Trans people can't be subject to the same law that governs Republicans. How else will they know that they are different, and therefore worse, than God's precious conservatives?

Using the restroom is one of the most vital and intimate functions that a person engages in during the course of an average day. It requires privacy, respect, and a certain level of solitude. But Republicans realize that. Almost every oppressive society in history has restricted people's ability to use the restroom freely. It is a unique and effective way of exerting control over your enemies, and naturally Republicans have become quite adept at it. Blacks once couldn't use the same restrooms as whites and now trans people can't use restrooms that correspond to their gender identity. Conservative ideals governed both of these decisions, and they clearly elucidate a trend.

Rather than cherishing personal liberty, as they usually claim to, Republicans stand in the way of this basic and rudimentary freedom that most people enjoy. Put yourself in the shoes of a trans women who needs to use a public restroom. Republicans have made it so that you may have a hard time using the women's restroom without getting arrested and thrown in jail. So, you would naturally opt to do the thing that can keep you from being incarcerated. But if you are wearing stereotypically female clothes, you won't be welcome in a men's room, either. Do you see? Republicans have made it virtually impossible for trans people to use the restroom at all without fear of being kicked out of the restroom, arrested, or both.

Republicans care so much about actively oppressing and harming trans people that they even place a substantial burden upon the precious businesses that they so wish to protect. It should be abundantly clear that Republicans do not have any true loyalties, even to those that they usually support. In order to provide adequate facilities to their customers and not alienate their trans customers, businesses are forced to build unisex bathrooms at a substantial cost to the bottom line of the business. These policies help literally no one. All they serve to do is subjugate a particular group of people whose existence Republicans have historically hated and bemoaned. If you can't keep people from being who they are, you have to resort to making sure that their lives are uncomfortable in almost every way you can control, even down to the most minor detail. Republicans have turned this into something of a professional sport at this point. But, then again, who is surprised? This is what Republicans do best.

They can't even admit that being transgender is a legitimate identity. Many, if not most, conservatives hold firm to the idea that there are only two genders, that gender is not fluid, and that to the extent that someone falls outside the binary, they are mentally or otherwise ill. The reality of the situation is that transgender people suffer from a disproportionately high occurrence of negative treatment and social outcomes. But this is hardly due to the fact that they are transgender. It is due to the fact that people make life so hard for them. People actively root for them to suffer and fail, and Republicans are marching in unison at the front of that parade. They support the right of employers to refuse to hire trans people. They support trans people being removed from schoolteacher positions. They deny that a person can be born with a legitimate gender identity that does not conform to their biological sex. Republicans may as well be living in the Stone Age.

Republican policies have real-world consequences in the lives of most trans people. Conservatives have made it incredibly difficult for trans people to get their gender designation changed on their driver's licenses. This is a crucial barrier between most trans people and open identification with their true gender identity. But the Republican position makes sense if you understand the goal of their policies. They don't want trans people to be taken seriously in society because they're not cis, white men. To the extent that they can block any sort of progress for this community, you can be sure that conservatives will pursue any and all avenues available to them. Why should a person care what someone else's driver's license says? It doesn't affect anyone but the holder of the license. But it does serve as a way to dictate the way that trans people live their lives and interact with society. That's the hook for Republicans. It's a way to dominate someone who is different than them. That's irresistible.

Conservatives can't even call trans people by the pronouns they prefer. Their rationale is that there are "proper" pronouns for biological men and women regardless of the person's gender identity. This is the height of selfishness and disregard for your fellow human being. They refuse to use trans people's preferred pronouns because <u>they</u> think it's wrong. That would be like saying "You're asking me to call you 'Tim', but you really seem like more of a 'Steve'. Since I think your name should be Steve, I'm going to call you that." It's a fundamental sign of disrespect, and it deserves to be treated as such. If you hear Republicans doing this, don't treat it as a mere difference of opinion. Treat them the way you would treat someone who yells at wait staff or cuts someone off on the freeway on purpose. Make them feel shame for the way that they treat people, and curtail your associations with them until they change their ways. This is literally the least they can do to contribute to societal progress.

Do not get this confused. Republicans do not view transgender people as human beings. In their minds, trans individuals are not deserving of the same rights that all humans have, let along the rights that most Americans enjoy. These are people who sympathize with judges that deny parental rights to trans parents based on the presumption that trans parents are unfit. Maybe courts should start presuming that Republican parents are inherently unfit. Maybe then they'll get a taste of what it really means to be a second-class citizen in this country. If Republicans were treated with half the disrespect that trans people experience every day, they would advocate for changes in the law so fast it would make your head spin. If they couldn't get housing, employment, or adequate health care, maybe they would come to understand what progress really means to those living in difficult circumstances. Who know? Maybe the tables will turn on Republicans one day, and we can tell them all "We told you so."

Finally, the Republican cause against all the members of the LGBT acronym ends with the only letter remaining, "B". Republicans deny the very existence of bisexuals. To them, bi people are "confused" or "greedy" sexual deviants who can't make up their minds about what they really want in life. In their minds, all bi people want to do is have sex with every adult they can get their hands on, and there's no good reason to let your children interact with them lest bi people infect them with their perverse ideals. In many cases, Republicans are closeted gay or bisexual people themselves. Perhaps this is all borne out of a combination of hate, envy, and regret. Maybe the most vicious anti-LGBT advocates are themselves deeply, deeply closeted. It would make sense, and I have no reason to think it's not true unless I hear evidence to the contrary. Your move, Republicans.

This very long chapter was meant to show that the differences between Democrats and Republicans are not merely political. People's lives are on the line. Until a few years ago, individuals could not marry the person they loved if that person was of the same sex. That right is younger than the smartphone, and it's already under threat of reversal. We have to resist Republicans at every turn, or else they will erode every right of non-straight, white, cis, rich men until there is nothing left. They're used to this position. They occupied it until minorities and women stood up and demanded that their voices be heard.

We cannot stop working and we cannot stop fighting. Every time a Republican wins an election, the alarm bells of oppression and injustice should ring in your head. That's a call to action, and it's up to you to answer it. If you don't, there's no telling when your rights will be on the chopping block. Only this time, there won't be anyone left to help you, because Republicans will have already decimated the legitimacy and existence of all those who at one point would stand up to defend you. The stakes are far too high for you to remain silent or complicit. We need all the help we can get, and it starts with you.

12

SOCIAL SECURITY AND ENTITLEMENTS

Most Republicans have no idea what it means to live on the economic margins of society. They have never had to struggle to figure out where their next meal will come from, how next month's rent will be paid, or how the latest medical bill will be paid. The vast majority of them come from backgrounds of extreme privilege, and they use that privilege in order to keep people of lesser means in their place. These are the ideals that most Republicans were raised with, and we can't expect them to change any time soon. In their eyes, financial opportunity and affluence make up a zero-sum game. Every time a poor person gets a leg up in society, a rich person loses out on an additional sum of money. To Republicans, this is the height of evil and injustice, and they will do anything they can to fight back against it.

Almost every prosperous society has measures in place to take care of their poor. They realize that in order to create large numbers of rich people, others often become poor in comparison and cannot afford to live in a society with elevated standards of living. Redistributing wealth and providing for social programs is the gold-standard treatment for this economic ailment, and many, many developed countries have employed it to date. In order for the programs to be successful, tax revenue must be received from industry or the citizenry to provide funding. This is one of the first reasons why Republicans stand against social entitlement programs. They don't want to give any of their precious money to assist the poor, despite the fact that income inequality very often results due to the prosperity that they have managed to achieve in life. It is an uncharitable and disgusting stance, but anti-tax language has become the lingua franca of the modern-day conservative.

But I've already discussed income inequality in an earlier chapter. Here, I want to focus on specific entitlement programs, why they are important, and why Republicans are reprehensible people for opposing them in the way that they do. Specifically, I want to have a concrete discussion regarding Social Security and similar programs designed to assist the poor. These social initiatives have been a part of the American fabric for decades, and Republicans simply want to rend them fiber by fiber until they are of no use to anyone. This is all, of course, so that they can keep more of their precious money and ensure that poor people never have a chance at stable food supplies, housing, and income, let alone a chance at climbing the social ladder.

To Republicans, the social ladder is not something that everyone has the opportunity to climb with hard work and dedication. Rather, it is a game of king of the hill, and Republicans have put countless amounts of time and resources into defending their position atop the hill of greed and capital gain. This is a toxic byproduct of extreme capitalism and amassing of money and power. Part of defending the hill means keeping any part of the hill from being compromised. To conservatives, this means that no money can be taken from the great, grandiose, golden hill to be used for those who can barely even view the hill from a distance. Progressives tried to take some of the land surrounding the hill, and have been staunchly rebuked at every attempt to expand their territory.

The golden goose of social entitlement programs in this country is Social Security. The average American has incredibly sparse retirement savings, in large part due to the incredibly high cost of living in many regions of the country and wages that have not kept up with inflation and increases in the cost of living. In order to ensure that Americans would be able to live well as they age and move into retirement, the Social Security system was developed to ensure a steady stream of income for retired workers. Of course, as the system becomes bigger and the administrative costs broaden, a larger tax base is needed to support it. But Republicans staunchly oppose any expansion of Social Security, and would prefer to see it privatized or eliminated entirely. This is largely because they don't want to have any more money taken out of their payroll taxes to fund the program.

The litany of problems with the Republican stance on this issue is too large to list in its entirety in one volume. But I would like to discuss some of the more glaring issues with it. First, it's important to bracket this discussion with the overall reason why Republicans want to gut Social Security. There are two tenets of the Republican platform, discussed at length throughout this book, that are satisfied by advocating against Social Security. First, gutting Social Security allows the rich to keep more of their money, despite the fact that it's not really enough money to make much of a difference in their lives. The rich will continue to be rich, Social Security or not. But they have to continue to try to line their pockets any way they can. If they don't do that, they really don't have any reason for living, do they?

Second, seeking to destroy Social Security allows Republicans to keep the poor in their place. Specifically, it allows them to keep poor, old people in their place. Keep in mind, Republicans do not care about old people unless they are rich. In the conservative mindset, if you make it to old age without abundant financial resources, you have failed somehow. So, they do not believe that they have any reason to care about you. Your poverty is your fault, and they have no societal obligation to make up the difference. Society gave them nothing. Nobody ever gave them anything. Every Republican believes that they are self-made and that this country never gave them anything except a hard time for being wealthy. They do not care about you and they never will. I know that I must sounds like a broken record at this point, but that's the core theme of this book. Republicans are incredibly annoying by their very existence. The point of their lives is to destroy any hope of success for anyone who is not white, rich, male, and straight. They should annoy all of us, simply by existing.

But, ideology aside, there is one glaring reason why Republicans really do not have any reason to complain about Social Security. The people who care the most about gutting Social Security are rich people who care about lowering their own tax burden. But most uber-wealthy people don't even pay the tax that directly goes to support Social Security. The program is funded largely through payroll taxes. Most rich people don't pay payroll taxes on most of their income since their wealth increases through higher share prices, corporate valuations, and capital gains, none of which are subject to payroll taxes. If anyone has the right to complain about Social Security, it's the middle class. We are the ones who pay for Social Security through payroll taxes withheld from our checks every two weeks. But we are okay with it because we have decided that it is worth it. We have decided that we want elderly people of all income brackets to have a reliable source of income at retirement, even if we have to pay a few more dollars per paycheck to make that a reality. In short, get out of our way, Republicans. We care about our nation's poor, even if you would rather step on their necks with your golden boots.

As if not caring about old people wasn't enough for Republicans, they also advocate for drastic reform of the food stamp system to eliminate what they perceive as waste from fraud and general abuse by the poor. Keep in mind, these are the same people that advocated bailing out big banks during the 2008 recession after they incurred substantial losses due to gambling depositor money. But, yes, poor people are the ones who are wasting our money. If the fact that most rallying cries against the food stamp system as we currently know it have come from Republicans is not enough to convince you that Republicans are an incredibly evil and heartless group of individuals, I'm not sure what is. We're talking about poor people who are food insecure and, in many cases, actually starving to death. Despite America's image as a portly and resource-abundant nation, there is a substantial minority of people in this country who do not have enough to eat. Even the people who have access to some sort of food only have access to nutrient-sparse food that itself contributes to obesity. Food stamp programs seek to solve both of these issues, but apparently that's not enough for Republicans to get on board.

Countless Republicans and conservative advocates have called for food stamp reform. From drug-testing welfare and food stamp recipients to restricting food choices for those who enroll in these programs, there seems to be no limit to Republicans' collective campaign to trim the fat from the leanest game animal in politics. Make no mistake, without these programs, people will starve to death in the streets. It's almost as though Republicans are fine with people starving to death in the streets if they can keep another dollar for themselves. To them, no poor person ever deserves a single public dollar for food. Any public benefit to be given to a poor person needs to be scrutinized with a more powerful lens than has ever been used on a rich person or a corporation.

Republicans won't stand for poor people having cell phones or eating shrimp cocktail on their dollar. This is likely because the rich are saving their dollars for corporate welfare and the government bailout of large businesses that fail after they cause recessions. It's easily demonstrable that Republicans care more about rich people than they do about poor people, and this glaring hypocrisy proves the argument more than anything else. Republicans want tax cuts until their taxes can benefit a rich person who needs a bailout. But as soon as a poor person needs a helping hand, conservatives will rip the rug out from any attempt at assistance so quickly that it'll make your head spin. These are not good people. These are people who demonstrate sociopathic behavior and possess no discernible moral norms or principles. They want rich, white men to thrive and everyone else to suffer. If we do nothing, they will get their way, and we all will be slaves to their whim sooner rather than later. This could, perhaps, happen literally.

To top off the trifecta of evil Republican obstinance, it's important to discuss conservative opposition to subsidized housing. In the Republican mindset, poor people who rely on public housing programs for shelter are freeloaders who are simply trying to get something for nothing. In reality, many of these people are attempting to escape difficult circumstances, raising children in single parent households, or holding down multiple jobs with too much month left at the end of the money. Yet, as soon as a new Republican presidential administration takes charge, they seek to raise rents in public housing to push people out and back into adverse economic circumstances. This is another classic example of Republicans trying to kick people while they are down. They sincerely believe that people want to stay in public housing longer than they need to just to avoid getting a job. Have you seen most public housing complexes? The only thing that causes people to get out of public housing faster than Republican politicians is the actual condition of the housing complexes themselves. Many of these clusters form so-called housing "projects" where crime, drug use, and domestic violence run rampant. People don't want to stay in these buildings one minute longer than they want to. Republicans refuse to face facts and admit they're wrong. They'd rather stick it to poor people any chance they get.

I could go on and on regarding the subject of social security and public entitlements. To the extent that America has any social programs designed to assist the less fortunate, you can be sure that Republicans oppose it. These are people who could not care less about the fate and well-being of poor people. Often, Republicans are only a few generations removed from extreme poverty themselves. But that's all it takes. Once their great-grandparent or great-grandparent made it out of poverty and achieved success through a combination of hard work and luck, it was only a matter of time. All it takes is a generation or two before maintaining wealth is all that one cares about, particularly if one has any conservative inclinations. It's a slippery slope to full-blown Republicanism from there.

13

RELIGION

Republicans cling to guns, money, and religion more than they cling to almost anything else in their lives. They do this for ultimately selfish reasons, but their priorities usually boil down to one or more of these three things. I've discussed guns and money elsewhere in this book. But I would be remiss to omit an examination of the Republican obsession with religion. After all, it explains so much about why Republicans act in the reprehensible ways that they do.

Conservatives in America are predominantly, but not exclusively, Christians. As a result, I will focus on the role that Christianity plays in Republican politics. Christianity is a unique religion in that many interpretations of the central texts and dogmas can be twisted and shuffled around to support a diverse array of interests. This is, of course, not true Christianity. Christianity, like the vast majority of religions, is a beautiful expression of personal belief, tolerance, and a desire for harmony with one's fellow human beings. I do not mean to say anything negative about Christianity in and of itself. However, what Republicans have done to Christianity and its popular perception is neither holy nor acceptable. So many Christians are wonderful and accepting people who only want to do the will of their creator. I am not talking to them or about them. I'm talking about those who use this religion to justify greed, oppression, and bigotry. With that caveat in place, let's get into more specifics.

The GOP uses religion in order to defend most of its horrific policies. Many, if not most, Christian denominations staunchly oppose abortion. Roman Catholicism is perhaps the most vocal of these. In order to support a position that abjectly harms and denigrates women, Republicans hold firm to the perspective of many Christian denominations that life begins at conception. This is not because Republicans are particularly devout or pious people. They hold firm to this stance because it just so happens to further their aim of taking rights away from women. They want to keep women in their place, and a particular religious stance allows them to call upon the divine to defend their position. It's all too convenient.

If Republicans cared about religion as much as they claim to, they would follow all the tenets of their religion regardless of how it would cause them to be perceived politically. Instead, they have positioned themselves as the epitome of "cafeteria Christians". They pick and choose the beliefs they will follow and those that they won't. They'll prioritize a clump of cells over the welfare of a woman, but they'll fight and argue against welfare programs despite the fact that their lord and savior calls upon them to help the less fortunate. Republicans cling to their money and scoff at public attempts to feed, clothe, and shelter the poor. Instead, they advocate for the exact opposite of what their scriptures call for. They work their tails off to ensure that rich, white men can horde money and keep it within a relatively small sphere of influence. It would be interesting to see how they will be viewed at the "pearly gates" they claim to believe in.

If you look at a particular part of Christian dogma and attempt to discern whether Republicans will adopt or disown it, all you have to do is look at who that particular tenet serves the most. Odds are, if it can be spun to serve rich, white men, it will be. Republicans have used religion to argue against everything from violent video games and drug use to abortion and welfare. This is an inherently twisted and mangled version of Christianity that serves only to keep the rich

rich and the poor poor. Republicans conveniently ignore that whole bit about the rich man having a harder time getting into heaven as a camel does of going passing through the eye of a needle. It's easy to forget that part when compulsively amassing wealth and fortune feels so much better than actual compliance with your own religious prescriptions.

The problem with Republicans and religion is that the vast majority of the GOP doesn't actually believe in anything greater than themselves. Religion is largely cultural to these people. You could not be a true Christian and behave the way that Republicans do. They act directly against the command to "love your neighbor as you love yourself". To the GOP, "as you love yourself" clearly means "strip yourself of wealth and systematically oppress yourself". If that rule were actually made of gold, Republicans would try to steal it from the rest of us and keep it for themselves. Do not believe their lies anymore. Republicans care about religion as much as they care about anything else. It only matters insofar as it can help them maintain their positions of affluence and social superiority over the rest of us. They are hypocrites and they deserve to be treated as such.

Take, as a further example, the oft-cited Christian commandment to preserve human life. As mentioned earlier, scripture and church teaching surrounding this maxim is used to defend the Republican position concerning abortion. If you fervently believe that life begins at conception, and are willing to apply that principle to human lives across the board, then your perspective is at the very least consistent. We can all understand the desire to preserve life, even if we disagree on the issue of when life begins. But Republicans can't even claim this kind of consistency. Their own opinions regarding the **value of human life** are incredibly self-contradicting and hypocritical. All one needs to do is look at the Republican perspective on the death penalty to see this glaring inconsistency. How can one claim the mantle of religion when it comes to early-stage fetuses but ditch it by the wayside when it comes to people convicted of crimes? As we've seen, two-faced belief comes rather easy to Republicans.

Let's look at another example. As discussed above, Republicans, being mostly Christian, subscribe to the idea that the most important commandment is to love thy neighbor as thyself. But this commandment goes out the window when it comes to treating immigrants like human beings. Republicans and their politicians will gladly rip a crying baby from the hands of a scared mother fleeing persecution in her native country, throw that baby in a cage, and prosecute the mother as a criminal under American law. How, exactly, is that treating thy neighbor as thyself? If a Republican found himself stranded on an icy road in a winter storm and used a nearby home for shelter while the storm passes, they would hardly expect to have their children taken from them and locked up in repurposed big-box store. They would expect a pat on the back and a mug of hot chocolate for their trouble. These people barely possess the baseline level of empathy required to be a human being, let alone a devout Christian.

There is one final example of the extreme problems that Republicans have when it comes to religion, although there are numerous others that different volumes can go through in more detail. The GOP has long been the party of so-called "religious liberty". That's basically a euphemism for "let me use my religion to oppress others while claiming oppression if anyone disagrees with me". It's a sickening perversion of the term "liberty". But Republicans don't even believe in religious liberty for those who are not Christian. They have been very vocal in their disdain for Muslims and everything having to do with Muslim culture. In fact, many of them have gone so far as to say that they want a ban on Muslims entering the United States. To support their perspective, they cite the "War on Terror" and essentially spout arguments that all end in some variation of "9/11 was bad." It is the height of self-preference, bigotry, and disingenuous thinking to hide under the veil of "religious liberty" while at the same time wanting to ban an entire religion of people from this country just because they pray to a different god. The Republican perspective on Muslims is hateful and they should be ashamed of themselves. Yet they claim that Christians are the true victims of discrimination and disdain in this country. Every year, they fabricate a "War on Christmas" while waging a literal war on Islam and Muslims all over the world. This should disgust any decent person.

There are countless examples of Republican hypocrisy when it comes to religious devotion. But they all have something in common. Conservatives use religion to justify beliefs that they would have held anyway. They are simply out to protect rich, straight, white men and to oppress everyone else. Christian institutions (as opposed to the religion itself) have historically favored this class of people over women and minorities. It's no surprise that Republicans feel right at home there, then. Rather than using Christianity as a vehicle for peace and unity, they use it as a means to keep others down and prevent anyone from ascending the social ladder to success and prosperity.

14

THE ENVIRONMENT

Like many crucial political issues, the health and well-being of the environment is a topic of discussion on which there would ideally be very little disagreement. We are all impacted by the environment because it affects us and everything we do. We cannot exist without an intact environment, and none of our life's work can occur without that dome of protection watching over us. Our lives and welfare come from the environment, and there is literally not enough we can do to repay it for creating and nurturing us.

But humans uniquely have been more of a scourge to the environment than any other species in history. Unlike other species, we have the ability to harm the environment intentionally, and we usually do. From ripping a hole in the ozone layer with acrid, disgusting chemicals to poisoning lakes and rivers with various colors of manufacturing runoff, humans are a cancer on the otherwise beautiful face of our planet. When we looked at the issue long enough to wake up and realize the horror that we had wrought on the environment, various plans were devised to mitigate our misdeeds. Naturally, these strategies required a substantial amount of legislation to ensure that everyone would comply. Policy without an enforcement mechanism is a wish, after all.

Where there is legislation, there are political parties. In this country, where there are political parties involved, Republicans inevitably emerge as one of a few dominant forces and seek to ruin everything for everyone else. The debate surrounding environmental policy is no exception. Even when the goal is to protect the atmosphere and the environment that we all live in and benefit from, Republicans have to make sure that any policy exclusively favors rich, white men. No law is valid in the eyes of conservatives if it does not satisfy these goals.

The Republican stance on environmental policy explicitly favors corporations, which are the bastion and stomping grounds of privileged white men. Rich white men are forged in corporations, and ultimately become one with these evil entities as they snake the tendrils of their influence through governing boards and controlling shareholder positions. Anything that remotely threatens the profits and power of these global behemoths threatens the rich, white man himself. Environmental policy had a small effect on the gargantuan, gluttonous profits that these companies have enjoyed since their founding. Naturally, Republicans needed to rally the troops to fight back.

Conservatives have opposed real environmental reform at every turn because corporations largely make their profit by treating the environment as their own private dump. Manufacturing plants render lakes flammable and trucks choke Mother Earth with smog as they carry load after load of material excess to the hands of people manipulated to want more and more. All the while, corporations reap the profits and satisfy their shareholders, making rich, white men even richer. It's a Republican fantasy in its purest form. It even has a greater upside for conservatives than allowing them to print and horde money from their ill-gotten and ill-operated enterprises. The landscape that existed before the advent of environmental law essentially allowed corporations to push the negative consequences of their actions onto poor people and minorities.

Rich, white men are not going to let anything affect the things they hold dear, even if those potential obstacles are the direct results of their own greedy and immoral actions. They hole their families up in gated communities with private security while they dump runoff through lakes and rivers that provide a water supply for the rest of us. They abandon barrels of poisonous chemical by-products near the homes of poor people, praying that the inevitable cancer that results cannot be tied to their nefarious ends. Without environmental legislation, this world persists and kills more and more of us every year. Rich, white men make out like the bandits they are, all for a few cents to be added to share prices.

Since we wanted to survive through the next century without choking to death on our own collective waste, legislatures passed moderate laws designed to disincentivize the pollution that had become so commonplace over the previous half-century. Very little was actually banned. Corporations just had to comply with pre-designed measures to ensure that their very existence did not poison the rest of us, as it does in so many other ways. They flew into a frenzy and dedicated oodles of money to lobbying for these very basic regulations to be rolled back, if not eliminated entirely. Lawyers were brought in to challenge every statute and agency action. One wonders how much it would have cost these evil entities to just comply with the regulations in the first place. I suspect the math would surprise us all.

The anti-environmental initiative took many forms. But perhaps the most despicable of all was the rise of climate change denial in general. Humans can't be responsible for changing their environment if global temperature changes are non-existent or random. If you can't take responsibility, then there's no reason for you to change your behavior. This is exactly the paradigm that Republicans espoused for decades. The malignant climate change denial mentality spread across the country and engulfed millions in its delusion. Republicans became the metastasis of the cancer that humans have been for the planet as a whole. No reform ever came without a fight, and long-term political strategies were devised solely in order to modify or eliminate this reform, all to favor big business. Your government sold you out, and you should treat them accordingly the next time you go to the polls.

Republicans want to poison the environment for increased profits, all while pushing any immediate detriments to minorities and the less privileged. This is eminently demonstrable in their continued lobbying against increased environmental regulation. But why would they do this? They have to live in the environment, too. The answer is quite simple. Republicans know that most effects of climate change and environmental degradation are not immediate. As far as they are concerned, the individuals making these decisions will be dead before the consequences of our misdeeds come to a head. They lack the foresight to even care about their children and grandchildren. That's what happens when you proclaim to be wholly self-made when you are the product of luck and privilege. You leave your descendants to perish under the greenhouse dome you constructed in Earth's atmosphere. If you're a Republican, what do you care? You're already dead.

Like so many issues that result in Republicans fleeing toward the wrong side of history, this problem has a very clear answer. Environmental regulation will not destroy big business. It will wipe a very small percentage off their balance sheet, but this will not result in a great loss of wealth. The choice is very simple for anyone with a soul. But that's just the problem: Republicans are absolutely soulless people who only care about the fortunes and profits of rich, white men. From their perspective, they can always buy their way out of the problem. They can pay for a house with a strong air conditioner if it gets too hot outside from that gaping hole in the ozone layer. They can buy water purifiers and bottled drinking water when they've poisoned their latest lake. All that matters is their bottom line. That's how it's always been and that's how it always will be.

But you have the ability to stand up for the environment through a very simple set of actions. Just vote these garish people out of office. They are soulless, humorless husks of human beings who have no capacity to see the world from outside their own screwed up points of view. Their actions are not meant to help find their next meal where they would otherwise starve. If it were, it would be moderately more understandable. However, this is purely to maintain profits to present to shareholders. It is the epitome of greed and evil selfish thinking. These boorish trolls try to pass off their anti-environmental advocacy as being better for the economy or for common investors.

Don't let these tricks fool you. If you are not a rich, white man, Republicans want you to burn to death under the fiery sun of deregulation. They will make off with the profits garnered from every iota of increased suffering foisted upon you by the business entities designed to perpetuate the privilege of white men in America. The only thing that can stop them is focused collective action. Unfortunately, the ball is in our court now, and we can't afford to let it bounce by. Our lives and the lives of our children are literally on the line. It's time we started acting like it.

15

WHITE PRIVILEGE

How many times have you heard successful people call themselves "self-made"? How many times have you heard those same people say that it's "all about hard work" and that they "didn't get where they are by luck"? There is a pervasive mentality in this country that gumption and fortitude can result in success without any underlying privilege or luck. You hear this sort of talk primarily among conservatives and Republicans, almost all of whom are white men. This is not a coincidence.

White men have occupied a unique place of privilege ever since they arrived on this continent and systematically committed genocide on our native population. When your race rapes and murders the people who were here before you and then spends centuries crafting and honing a system of laws and customs that exclusively benefits you, there is no doubt that you enjoy a substantial amount of privilege. White people did all this and more. Most liberal white people acknowledge their privilege and leave it at the door when entering into conversations with oppressed minority groups. This chapter, as you may have guessed, is not for them. Rather, this chapter is meant to address Republicans, who refuse to admit that they have any privilege. Their myopic nature is, yet again, shown to be in full bloom through this belief. Let's take a closer look.

White people enjoy advantage in virtually every aspect of American life. From educational opportunities to interactions with police officers, white people make off better in almost every category than people of color. Republicans take these statistics and spin them as correlations without causation. They say it's not their fault that they enjoy a higher social status than people of color. They claim that they cannot control the way society views them, and that racial preference has no bearing on one's ability to succeed in this country. It's an absolute crock. The trust is that the vast majority of wealthy people in this country are white. They became successful due to a combination of privilege, luck, and work, as I discussed earlier. But Republicans refuse to believe that the first two factors have any bearing on their success.

It is not difficult to show how their argument is utterly and completely asinine. If you look at life as a road with a series of exits and potholes, it's easy to demonstrate that the vast majority of white people, particularly white people with money, have it far easier than people of color. This is true even when the person of color has money. Whiteness is just that powerful. If life is a two-lane road, one of those lanes is pristine and meticulously maintained. Generations of effort, money, and influence have gone into making sure that lane is devoid of potholes, debris, and obstacles. Any time an issue is reported with the road, every driver lucky enough to have been assigned to that lane stops what they're doing to ensure that the nuisance is dealt with quickly. Traffic resumes in that lane almost as quickly as it is stopped, and it will be quite some time before any substantial issue presents itself with that lane again. There are exits at every mile of this road, all of which lead to incredibly decadent hotels that only those drivers can use. These hotels provide a welcome respite from the day's drive, and allow the drivers to lay their head on plush pillows in well-appointed beds. It's quite the life.

Contrast this with the other side of the road. This side of the road has so many issues that it's almost not worth traveling. There are potholes everywhere, and there are construction crews every few miles that lead to miles-long backups. The potholes break crucial components of cars all the time. Sometimes they lead to accidents that kill drivers. There's trash all over the place, most of it thrown there by drivers on the other side of the road. In fact, when those other drivers find trash on their road, they all get together and make sure that it is thrown on the bad side of the road. Why should they care? At least it's off their side of the road. With so many breakdowns, it would be helpful to have nice hotels to stay in until rescue and repair crews can come. But there are no hotels off this road. There are no rescue and repair crews, either. People on the other side of the road just don't understand how these drivers fail to reach their destination. All they have to do is drive, after all.

White people occupy the easy side of the road. They didn't build the road. It was built for them, and kept in perfect working order for generations before them. Each of them has to exert minimal effort to keep that side of the road the way it is, but the integrity of the road means more than anything. The white side of the road leads to success. They've constructed nice hotels for themselves that take the form of generational wealth, corporate connections, and lack of taxation on various forms of affluence. It's a great side of the road as long as everyone does their part to maintain it.

Every non-white person occupies the other side of the road. Nobody took the time or effort to make sure that it could stand up to the wear and tear of such consistent use. Everyone with money used it for the upkeep of the white side of the road. Potholes developed over time, and nobody had the resources to fix them. In fact, sometimes these potholes would kill you. These potholes took the form of police violence, low-income housing, and disparate access to healthy food. The trash that litters the street mostly came from the white side of the road. That trash is white indifference to the suffering of people of color, corporate profits made off the backs of brown people, and the lack of people of color in influential places in corporate America. Worse yet, there are consistent large obstacles that keep anyone from getting down the non-white side of the road. These obstacles are systemic racism, overt prejudice and discrimination, and denial of opportunity based on race and ethnicity. There are no hotels on this road because no one will give people of color a break.

There is a large median separating the two sides of the road. The median is so tall that no one can ever hope to cross it, but not tall enough that the drivers on each side of the road can't see each other. It is made up of American culture. Culture is what divides us into haves and have-nots based on the color of one's skin. The median can be destroyed, but almost no one is interested in that, particularly on the white side of the road.

Republicans claim that there is only one road and that we are all just drivers. If we just shut up and drive as opposed to complaining about the potholes that only seem to be in our path, then maybe we can succeed. They point to the infinitesimal fraction of incredibly skilled drivers that do happen to make it down the rough side of the road as evidence that everyone should be able to do it. Republicans invent fictional potholes and say that they managed to drive over them without issue. In reality, those are mere divots in the road that will quickly be remedied by that crackerjack repair team you keep hearing about. In all fairness, it's hard to identify a true pothole if you've never really seen one. People of color keep offering to show them what a pothole really looks like so that they can know the true nature of the suffering that exists on the non-white side of the road. But Republicans keep insisting that all holes in the road look the same and affect all cars in exactly the same way. That way, they don't need to look for themselves.

This is why Republicans don't believe in privilege. They've never experienced the rampant discrimination and hatred that accompanies brown skin in this country. Why would they think it exists? They refuse to take it on faith like so many of our white liberal allies do. Conservatives legislate based on their own faith in their conception of a higher power, but they can't have faith in brown people's description of their own circumstances. They just ask why people of color can't take responsibility for the condition of the road and fix it of their own volition. Of course, they ignore the fact that they own the construction companies that have the power to actually fix the road. Instead, those companies spend time fixing the white side of the road and building hotels for white people to sleep in when they take one of the myriad exits along the road. Anyone who complains about the road is ignoring the real problem in the Republican worldview. If they just focused on fixing the road, they could get to success sooner. But the brown people refuse to do so, so they have to live with the condition of their roads.

Many Republicans go so far as to say that the condition of the not-white side of the road is the fault of brown people in the first place. They ignore the trash they threw, the obstacles they created and ignored, and the potholes that they contributed to. This criticism comes in the form of "black on black crime" arguments, as well as similar rhetoric designed to blame people of color for their own problems. It's truly a disgusting attitude. But Republicans don't care as long as the white side of the road remains pristine. That's their only interest, and they will pursue it at all costs.

Perhaps worst of all, Republicans refuse to admit that the collective action and resources that go into maintaining the white side of the road actually benefits them. Getting to success is a virtue of their skill and fortitude in driving, rather than their reliance on having a functional road to get them there. To them, having a nice road is not an advantage. Even if they do admit that there is some benefit, they say that it can't be responsible for the fact that they reach success faster and with less effort than those who are forced to drive on the non-white side of the road.

I recognize that this analogy is becoming somewhat strained, but it is important to realize that privilege has very little to do with the nature of success itself. We luckily live in a society where people of all colors and creeds can flourish. But the point remains that it is much easier for white people to attain success than it is for brown people due to the fact that society has been set up for them. It would be imprudent to blame individual white people for the existence of white privilege in the twenty-first century. However, refusing to admit that it exists or denying that it plays a role in the success of individual white people is insulting and intellectually disingenuous.

This is the platform to which Republicans have committed themselves. If something besides their talent and work ethic is responsible for their success, even in part, then their entire narrative of personal responsibility can be called into question. Without that, they would have a harder time justifying the denial of assistance and rights to Americans who would benefit from some additional help in life. Republicans dedicate themselves to oppressing and repressing anyone who is not a rich, white man. It becomes that much easier to do when conservatives spin the advantage that rich, white men enjoy as the product of personal endeavor rather than societal preference. It's truly evil and ignorant. But, then again, these are Republicans we're talking about here.

16

EDUCATION

A strong public education system is the backbone of any strong and influential nation. America as a collective has agreed that publicly-funded education is a crucial and necessary public good. In order to create an educated populace and ensure the competence of the next generation, we have to ensure that all Americans have equal access to education. Allowing schools and public education to become stratified along social lines permits the spread of the toxic ideals that created those lines in the first place. If that happens, we can never hope to truly advance as a country.

Liberals, of course, have always been champions of a strong, regulated public education system. They recognize, of course, that this system requires a large amount of money to survive. All liberals want is for the rich to pay their fair share to ensure that we receive the fruits of our collective promise to future generations. We want our kids to grow up better than we did, and that cannot happen without proficient public education and associated programs. Liberals have committed themselves to ensuring that our children do have these opportunities. Republicans, on the other hand, want to spread their evil message of social stratification and systemic oppression. Public education stands in the way of their goals, and so they seek to undermine it at every turn.

It is no secret that our public education system is incredibly damaged in many ways. From state education corruption scandals to the uselessness of federal officials and policy, no one think of the children when it comes to...well...educating children. Due to these flaws that have run rampant throughout the system, public education has become inferior to many forms of private education. This is not universally true, but there are strong trends that favor private education in most settings. Such a difference alone marks a difference between the haves and have-nots. If you can afford private education for your children, they will go on to earn better degrees and be considered for better jobs than those who could not. This is inherently unequal and unfair. It is antithetical to the American ideal.

The paradigm I have set out above is not universal. There are many areas of country where public schools are better than private schools. But the trends are what they are. Who would not send their kid to the best private school if they could afford to? That desire is why almost all rich people send their children to private schools. But the dichotomy between rich and poor schools is responsible for perpetuating income inequality, prejudice, and the lack of social mobility that all poison our society now more than ever. Republicans contribute to this scheme to a greater degree than any other demographic because it inherently benefits them and their children to do so.

Remember, Republicans care about oppressing and silencing anyone who is not a rich, white man. The chief means through which women and brown people can improve their lot in life is to utilize a good education to secure a good job. This is a direct threat to the Republican way of life. So, they ensure that the schools that minorities attend are underfunded and dangerous. If the infrastructure is falling apart, students can never hope to have the kind of stability necessary to foster young minds. Day after day, their chances of succeeding in the world slip away a little more. Not only can kids not pull themselves up by their own bootstraps (because, you know, they're kids), Republicans don't even want to provide them with bootstraps in the first place. These children are being given literally no chance to succeed. The outcome of the race is decided for them before the race even starts.

Conservatives use several different means to ensure that public schools, particularly in urban areas, remain inherently second-class institutions of learning. The primary method is funding or, more properly put, a lack thereof. By continually advocating against increased public spending in general, and specifically for schools, Republicans directly cast these children into the American underclass. They don't care, because these kids are not rich, white males. Precious, conservative tax dollars cannot be spent to ensure that a historically disparaged group can receive the public education that their parents and grandparents were denied due to legal discrimination and societal disdain. The racists and bigots of the past are being bolstered by the racist and bigoted Republicans of the present. The only way to right these historic wrongs is to ensure that the descendants of those who were targeted by the legal system have the same access to a good education as anyone else. By refusing to provide and increase the funding that is necessary to improve schools and to keep good schools afloat, Republicans are necessarily saying that they are okay with the scars of the past.

Why should we be surprised. Republican selfishness is a unique and easily understood evil. In order to create more people like them, they have to do everything they can to make sure that their children have everything they had and then some. This means sending them to private schools and making donations to those schools in the supposed name of making the world a better place. In reality, all they are doing is making the world of rich, white men a better place. Newsflash, it was already a pretty great place to start with. There's certainly nothing wrong with striving to better the position of your children. But intent matters. It is plainly and demonstrably clear that Republicans favor their own children at the expense of everyone else. Even this would be somewhat understandable if they did not actively work against the interests of anyone who is not a rich, white man.

They do not want anyone else to make it in this country. To Republicans, success is a zero-sum game, and if someone else's kid gains any ground, their own kids must lose something. It doesn't matter that this concept is patently false. These are not logical people we're dealing with.

Childhood is the most crucial time of a person's life. The habits and behaviors that we learn as children follow us through the rest of our lives and are incredibly hard to reverse or modify. We learn how to be people as children, and the quality of one's childhood can be directly tied to the kind of adult that one turns out to be. In order to make sure that our world has more good people in it, we need to make sure that children are surrounded by positive and enriching influences. But if a group could make it so that members of a particular group have worse childhoods, they could ensure that adults in that group cannot compete. This is exactly what Republicans want. They want women and brown people to suffer and to form a permanent underclass. Their practices are wholly intentional and make up a substantial part of systemic racism and violence in this country.

Republicans' campaign against public education and social mobility does not end with educating children. One of the few things that can help to overcome a somewhat negative primary and secondary school experience is a strong system of publicly funded post-secondary education. Simply put, we need free college opportunities for all. We cannot complain about having an undereducated populace when we refuse to provide the means necessary to mitigate the problem. But Republicans rally against any public support for post-secondary education at every turn. They do not want publicly guaranteed student loans, federally funded tuition programs, or government grants to support students of lesser means. Conservatives want college to go back to what it was in the past: a means for the rich to further educate themselves and claim a monopoly over high-paying careers. They don't want the middle and lower classes to have any opportunities to ascend the social ladder. The Republican view from the top is clearly too good to share.

Education cannot be subject to market forces because the end product is too attenuated from the process. This is what Republicans can't understand about education policy. It's easy to reduce anything to free market politics. When it comes to business and regulation of specific industries, the concept is fairly easy to explain and even easy to defend in certain instances. If you run a business making trinkets, your trinkets will cost less to make and will sell for a lower price than they would if you had to pay to comply with expensive and potentially useless regulations. But education is not a product. The only measure of the success of the educational system is the creation of a good student. Unfortunately, policy needs to be made now, and its difficult to predict what will work over the entirety of a given child's time in a public school system. There's no balance sheet that can show the success of a program as a child moves along. Schools do not collect revenue that is not used in some way to further the aim of educating children. There's no profit measure that can be used as a guiding measure. But the stakes are far higher than the quarterly earnings of some fancy corporation.

The welfare of America's children is at stake. You have a voice in how this country's future will be shaped. Luckily, corporations do not control public schools yet. But we need to keep that from happening. Remember, Republicans want to keep public schools down in order to make their private school educations mean more. They're not better than us. They're not smarter than us. They have not been chosen from on high. Do not let them perpetuate the lie that they have earned more than we have. Our children can and will one day stand alongside their children in the boardroom. All we need to do is fight back and furnish them with the equal ability and opportunity to make the most of their lives and fulfill their destinies.

17

MINIMUM WAGE

The topic of minimum wage is an offshoot of the discussion of income inequality. I've touched on that elsewhere in this book, but I wanted to briefly look at the specific issue of minimum wage laws as a unique example of the evil that Republican fiscal policy has unleashed on this country. Minimum wage laws are quite simple and serve a very specific purpose. As the cost of living increases, people need more money to make the most basic ends meet. This is common sense. The longer that the cost of living increases without an associated raise in the minimum wage, the more you see workers stuck in desperate and quasi-impoverished situations. The rise of welfare programs and public assistance can mitigate this disconnect. But the most basic way of guaranteeing that workers have the ability to pay rent and provide for their families is to have strong and commonsense minimum wage laws.

Republicans oppose these laws every time they are brought up in public or political discourse. They harp on about the need to "guarantee the freedom of employers". To them, the bottom line of major corporations means more than the life and well-being of American workers and their families. The truth is that minimum wage laws would not put much of a dent in the cherished profits of corporations. They can afford to pay these people more than they are paying them, and the only refuge that the workers have is the power of the government to step in and do what's right. Minimum wage laws save lives. They pay medical bills. They buy school clothes. They help start and bolster nest eggs.

Again, Republicans only care about their core base, which is rich, white men. Minimum wage laws fly in the face of the outrageously privileged position that rich, white men have oppressed so many people to attain. The laws take some, although not much, money out of the pockets of these scumbags and put it into the dwindling checking accounts of the workers that helped put their companies on the map. Without them, workers struggle to make a respectable living and feed their families. Minimum wage laws help everyone except those who are obsessed with skyrocketing corporate profits and share prices. Considering how much money this vocal minority makes, it's little surprise that they have been able to make it a debated issue as opposed to a obvious conclusion.

Opposing minimum wage laws is a way to keep the middle and lower classes in their "place". To Republicans, only members of the upper class are supposed to succeed. They view themselves as being inherently better than you and me. Only their children, their friends, and their friends' children deserve to stand alongside them in the pantheon of American greatness. Everyone else exists to serve them, and only to serve them. Republicans believe in an intrinsic and necessary system of haves and have-nots. Success is a zero-sum game, and anyone else's gain is their loss.

Since a robust minimum wage would allow middle-class wage earners and their children to have a better shot at living the American dream, Republicans have naturally dedicated themselves to opposing it. Like the leech's natural biological function is to suck blood, Republicans' natural function is to oppress and repress anyone who is not a rich, white male. It comes entirely too easy to them. Opposing minimum wage laws is a simple and overt way to show that you do not care about the workers of this country. Republicans scream it from the mountaintop. They got theirs, and they believe they bear no responsibility for assisting those who laid down and formed the path to success on which they trod years earlier.

Thanks to the few actual remains of true democracy in this country, you still have a voice. You can stand up and demand that your lawmakers fight for the rights of workers. Family trees are changed forever when the minimum wage is increased. Republicans may want to keep you under their boots and bind you to the chains of corporate masters for the rest of your natural-born lives. But the debate does not end there. You have a role in shaping your future and your destiny. You can stand up and scream your defiance in their faces the next time you go to the polls. Light up your representatives' phone lines and demand that the collective will of the workers be heard. Reject complacency and send a message that will cover Wall Street to Washington, saying that neither will be allowed to keep the American workers down any more. If you don't, the consequences of your inaction will not just be stagnation. You will continue to drift backwards until your work becomes literally worthless. Only then will Republicans actually think you deserve what they pay you.

18

HEALTH CARE

Crises involving health care can rend a family apart in many ways. Obviously, there is the immediate concern regarding your loved one's health. That is first and foremost. But, assuming that they pull through, you are often left with piles of medical bills that you can never hope to repay in an expeditious fashion. Entire industries have cropped up just to finance these ridiculous charges. The natural misgivings of the human body lead to financial indentured servitude that lasts for years, if not a lifetime. The primary concern of a patient should be to get better, not to get sicker by worrying about how they'll pay their massive debts once they leave the hospital.

America is in quite a unique position with respect to health care. We provide some of the highest quality health care services in the world. Our research labs and pharmaceutical development programs are among the best in the world. Patients come to the United States from all over the world for novel new treatments for debilitating illnesses. Yet no one but the rich and privileged can afford these services without wondering how they're going to pay for them. Many of us are fortunate enough to have health insurance coverage through our employers. However, even these plans often have incredibly high deductibles. Some of these deductibles are so high that they function like a bandage that only covers eighty or ninety percent of a wound. The wound won't heal without being totally covered and protected.

Other developed countries do not have it this way. They have socialized health care plans that ensure that the government makes a substantial and meaningful investment in the health care of its citizens. This usually takes the form of total health care coverage through government programs. Many countries make it so that residents do not have to pay anything out of pocket for most, if not all, health care services. The programs can only function with adequate funding, provided through revenue from taxation. It's an incredibly small price to pay to make sure that infant mortality decreases and that cancer does not bankrupt families. We would all pay something to this system under universal health care, and rich people would have to pay a little more since they've been incredibly privileged and fortunate to have so much money at their disposal.

This is where Republicans step in to ruin the day once more. Any program that threatens to take any of their money and use it for public good is quite the bee in their bonnet. I swear that Republicans would abolish public funding for roads if they could get away with it. Like almost all Republican positions, the importance of the good at issue has no relevance to whether they support it. It is undeniable that universal healthcare would have far more positive ramifications than negative ones. The only downside is that rich people and corporations would be forced to pay their fair share for a change. This would all be in exchange for health coverage for millions of Americans and an associated increase in the average quality of life. What an evil that would be.

Remember, as I have constantly been reminding you throughout this book, Republicans are good at two things and two things only: 1. Exclusively caring about the welfare of rich, white men and 2. Oppressing anyone who is not a rich, white man. That's it. That's all they want. They want nothing else. Like most of the Republican platform, their position on government-funded health care programs allows them to achieve both of their aims at once. Rich, white men would need to bear a large part of the cost of implementing universal health care programs, because they have more resources as a result of their societal privilege. Also, many of the beneficiaries of universal health care would be women and people of color. Since universal health care costs rich, white men something (albeit a drop in the proverbial bucket) and stands to help women and brown people, it stands to reason that Republicans abhor the very concept of it.

The common Republican arguments against universal health care involve not wanting to be forced to support the care of others and claiming that the quality of care would decrease if the government were to guarantee care for all its citizens. They also claim that single-payer health care would wreak havoc on the American economy and render public spending far too high to be sustainable. Further, they argue that the free market takes care of the cost of health care better than any government system could. Finally, they claim that universal health-care would categorically increase the cost of health care to the point where the charge for services would far exceed its intrinsic value and inherent cost to provide. All of these arguments hold absolutely no water and just go to show that Republicans will grasp at literally any straws in order to deny health care to their fellow Americans. Rather than taking an honest inventory of the vast range of pros and limited cons of implementing universal health care programs in this country, Republicans would rather use base reasoning in order to appeal to their piggish base that categorically refuses any call to empathy. It truly is a sickening way to live one's life.

Let's look at each of these arguments in turn. They each crumble rather easily. First, Republicans claim that being forced to support the care of others is somehow a negative thing. To them, each person should be solely and exclusively responsible for their own health care. It is akin to their classic "pull yourself up by your own bootstraps" argument, and it is exactly as strong as that old flimsy saw. The chief problem with this position is that it assumes that Republicans don't benefit from providing and funding communal goods. What are roads, after all, if not a public good funded by tax dollars from almost everyone who earns a salary or hourly wage? Rich people use roads all the time. Is that pulling yourself up by your own bootstraps? We don't force people to pay for their own roads, and we shouldn't force people to pay for their own cancer treatment when they plainly cannot afford to do so. Further, Republicans will also benefit from universal health care. That's what universal health care means. Everyone stands to gain something. This is not pure philanthropy. Republicans would be paying for their own health care, too! Even from their own twisted, selfish sense of right and wrong, Republicans really should be able to see the good in this type of social program.

Republicans would counter and insist that they can pay for their own health care and would rather continue doing things that way than pool their money to guarantee that everyone has access to care. This is a variation on the typical Republican theme of "I got mine. Why should I help you get yours?" The rebuke to this counterargument is simple and is best expressed in two parts. First, neither Republicans nor anyone else got anywhere on their own. We all exist and experience success due to the contributions and influence of those around us. Rich people get to work by driving on publicly-funded roads, take advantage of publicly-funded corporate welfare programs, and likely benefit from publicly-funded police forces that safeguard them and their families. Republicans, even the richest and whitest among them, benefit from collective resources that you and I have helped to fund. The argument that they got theirs and we need to get ours is therefore patently absurd. "Getting theirs" was not their own doing, so they need to help make sure that getting ours does not solely have to be our own doing.

Second, the entire argument is based in selfishness and antisocial thinking. It's no secret that Republicans fundamentally lack empathy, but this goes to an entirely new level. To say that you would rather hold onto your gobs of undeserved and excessive funds while a single mother dies of cancer when you could be part of the solution is a unique sort of evil. If you count yourself in this unfortunate camp, you should be completely ashamed of yourself. You are not a good person, and you cannot reasonably expect to be treated as such. That's all that needs to be said on that point.

The next Republican argument against universal health care is that the quality of health care would decrease under this kind of system. This usually consists of some variation of the so-called "tragedy of the commons" argument. Essentially, they claim that no public resource can be of the highest quality because people will use it freely and frequently, reducing the supposedly pristine nature of exclusive goods. Commonly cited examples of this phenomenon are public parks and city sidewalks, both of which become somewhat filthy and run down due to the sheer number people who avail themselves of their utility and convenience. However, it has been demonstrated that this would not happen under a universal health care system. Just look at Canada. Are people dying in hospitals left and right just because the government pays for the health care of all Canadian citizens? Clearly that's not the case. Canada still trains doctors well and provides quality care to its people. When you collect enough money to support this endeavor, it becomes a well-organized and well-administrated machine. Even though America has some of the highest quality health care services in the world, we are consistently rivaled by countries that have socialized health care systems. This goes to show that quality of care cannot be directly tied to whether a given health care system is funded by a single-payer system. Once again, the Republican argument falls apart.

Republicans also claim that universal health care would destroy the American economy by placing too great of a strain on the budget. They tie this to the inevitable increase in public spending that would come from instituting a universal health care policy in the United States. While spending would increase in order to guarantee that the program is adequately funded, this is just another way that Republicans avoid any policy that could chip away at their precious fortunes. Rather than living within their means like the vast majority of Americans do, Republicans want to cling onto their money with a cold, dead grasp. They do not understand the basics of a balance sheet. To them, the costs of health care will just keep increasing, and more money will be required to fund a universal health care system. The truth is that societies make programs work when there is a collective will to make them work. Republicans conveniently support the vast tax cuts they have been given. Those were not paid for, but they persisted because a strong and vocal group of people staunchly advocated for their existence. The same could be true of single-payer health care. The only difference is that Republicans would refuse to cooperate. It's like your kid saying that eating vegetables would never work because they'd never eat vegetables. If they ate their vegetables, they'd reap all the benefits. Then again, this is hardly the first time that Republicans have stymied beneficial social policy by acting like petulant children.

As more Republican arguments against universal health care fall to the piercing sword of logic, more pop up to fight for the futile cause of ignorance. Next in line is the lame contention that the free market can take care of the health care problem. In the Republican worldview, there is almost no issue that the free market cannot instantly improve. Regulation only drives up costs, worsens outcomes, and restricts the ability of new players to enter a particular arena of commerce. This is why Republicans want to privatize almost every social program. It means that they would not have to pay for anything to support their neighbor despite the fact that their neighbors have been paying taxes to support them. These are quite convenient arguments for Republicans to make because they can afford to pay for any benefits out of their own pockets. They do not need shared risk because they have the unique and rare ability to insure against most of their own catastrophes. Private market insurance is a drop in the bucket for these fat cats, and they cannot fathom how anyone would be unable to purchase it on their own. The problem with this argument is the same problem that many other free market problems have: There are many things that the free market renders less efficient.

Just like it would be incredibly inefficient for every power company to build their own power lines rather than running energy on heavily regulated lines in structured systems, health care cannot be subject to market forces. The stakes are too high and the cost of competition is far too severe. Free market private health care can work well when you don't live in a food desert, you have access to regular preventive health care services, and you have the money to comply with regular medication regimens. Most Republicans are wealthy enough to be healthy until they reach old age. They see great health care professionals throughout their childhoods, early adulthood, middle age, and their early golden years. Their longevity is limited only by their genetics and the current state of modern medicine. But they enjoy the reduced premiums that come from the lower risk that this privilege affords them. For the rest of us who have some sort of identifiable "preexisting condition" due to not being rich, the market is not nearly as forgiving. We need the law to compel rich people to pay their fair share to a system that supports them and allows them to accrue money at almost inhumane paces. This includes supporting the health care of those who have the misfortune of having to work for them due to the lack of a silver spoon in their mouth at birth. The market punishes these people and would force them to pay their last dime for health insurance premiums. We can't pretend that the free market would work here any more than it would work for roads. We have communal roads for a reason and we need universal health care for the same reason. We all need it and we all use it.

Last but certainly not least comes the common Republican contention that a universal health care programs would drive up the cost of health care services to the point where they no longer reflect the intrinsic cost of those services. This is essentially a way of saying that rapid inflation would swallow up the American health care landscape. Again, such an argument is based on the idea that something would happen just because they think we would allow it to happen. A regulated universal health care system would undoubtedly contain safeguards to ensure that the cost of health care services would not inflate above a set pace each year. We do the same thing with our monetary policy. Why would we not do so with our nation's health care policy? Republicans are likely correct that without such safeguards, health care costs could go the way of university tuition (yet another problem that could be fixed with socialized programs). As you can see, the Republican argument with respect to increasing health care costs holds no water, and there's no reason to engage it any further.

None of the Republican arguments against universal health care stand up to reason. They all fall apart rather easily. This is, of course, because Republicans do not take any of these positions in good faith. You make better arguments when you actually believe them. The real reason that Republicans refuse to allow universal health care to become the law of the land is that the policy does not actively help rich, white men, and allows for brown people to live longer and happier lives. Republicans do not want to pay for this. They'd rather hold onto their money and use it to enrich their cozy, privileged lives. So, the next time that you find yourself at the polls, ask yourself which candidate actually cares about your welfare and the welfare of your family. If the candidate on the page has an (R) by their name, rest assured that they could not care less about you. They would gleefully check the balance in their checking account while you die of cancer, leaving mountains of unpaid medical bills for your estate to deal with. At least rich, white men won't have had to pay for your care. Make the right choice.

19

CONFEDERATE LEGACY

As of the time of this writing, the Civil War ended over 153 years ago. The war was fought over what went down in history as one of the most open and shut moral issues in the entire span of human existence. Brothers fought over the right of rich, white men to own slaves. Blood was spilled, families were destroyed, and our nation's image was changed forever. It was a war that would not have needed to be fought if America had a functional moral compass at the time. Regardless, it happened and the right outcome was reached.

That is, of course, unless you are a Republican. Southern conservatives cling to Confederate legacy and rhetoric with a nearly unshakeable force. Many refer to the Civil War as the "war of northern aggression" and cling to the notion that "the South will rise again". When challenged on their ridiculous and insulting viewpoints, Republicans usually spout some combination of valuing free speech and saying that their Confederate nostalgia is a function of "heritage, not hate". It's all the feckless manifestation of a racist, hateful lineage of former slaveholders who honestly believe that something was taken from them.

There's a reason that Republicans are overwhelmingly influenced by Southern politics. They will not let the Civil War go. It was the single biggest event in the history of rich, white men. In four short years, they had a substantial amount of their earning potential rendered legally impossible and lost their ability to literally own brown people. Since fighting for the interests of rich, white men and oppressing minorities make up the two halves of the proverbial flag under which Republicans march, it's hardly a surprise that Confederate nostalgia persists.

Republicans seem to be continually engaged in a fight to make sure that the Confederate legacy persists in modern American society. Whether fighting for the stars and bars to remain part of state flags or marching in the streets when a town tears down a statue of a Confederate leader, their stance could hardly be clearer. They want to make sure that we never forget about the Confederacy and that we remember that it could always come back under the right conditions. That's exactly the outcome they want. They crave more than anything to return to a time when rich, white men were favored under the letter of the law, rather than just the spirit of the law. Republicans want America to return to one of its most horrid times, when black and brown people were property, or at the very least second-class citizens, legally barred from interacting with white people on threat of imprisonment. I believe they call those "the good old days".

This chapter does not need to be particularly long because the Republican position on this issue is abundantly clear. Don't let them fool you by claiming that this is an issue of heritage. Anything in the past can be characterized as a matter of heritage if you yell enough about it. This doesn't mean that particular part of one's past is anything worth being proud about. Confederate nostalgia is a plainer example of this phenomenon than almost any other. If you cling to the stars and bars and argue that the Confederacy was really about the spirit of rebellion, you are a racist and you deserve to be treated as such. The Civil War was fought over the right of rich, white men to own slaves. One side took up arms to defend that right and the other side fought to tear it down.

These are the sorts of cut and dry issues on which Republicans cannot be trusted to make the proper call. If we cannot trust them to say that the Confederacy was wrong for countless reasons, how can we trust them to govern? The simple answer is that we can't. Not only do Republicans long for the reign of a country that fought for the right to own slaves, they long for the reign of a country that seceded from the union that they claim to love so much. To them, black athletes kneeling is un-American, but sporting the Confederate flag on t-shirts, truck windows, and state emblems is just heritage. The entire concept is completely backwards. Don't elect people who long for a time when rich, white men ruled the world and owned other human beings. Vote for people who actually care about you and your family.

20

MENTAL HEALTH

Republicans base a substantial portion of their rhetoric on the ideas of personal responsibility and hard work. Many able-bodied people are duped by this ruse. They ignore the realities of privilege and structural violence against the people who are lower on the social ladder. But there is a notable exception to even the Republican ideals of accountability and bootstrap-pulling. How do people with mental illnesses fit in to their calculus.

Unsurprisingly, they don't. But the Republican position on mental health is arguably more callous than almost any of their other stances. Generally, conservatives are not willing to sacrifice the well-being of rich, white men due to the ramifications such precedent could have on the remainder of rich, white men that make up the Republican party. What affects one usually has the potential to affect all. But mental illness occupies a unique place in the Republican hierarchy. It signifies some inherent, potentially moral flaw that warrants removal from the upper echelon in which Republicans have ensconced themselves. In a sense, there's an odd bit of equality here. Republicans will ostracize even rich, white men with severe mental illness unless they can be clandestinely separated, treated, and reintegrated before anyone is the wiser.

Mental illness, while somewhat tied to privilege and social standing, does not discriminate per se. There are severely mentally ill people in every social stratum. Because mental illness is a physical process, no amount of money can eliminate it completely from the monied classes. This is what scares Republicans the most. No matter how much money or social advantage they have, they are a set of brain chemicals away from being completely outcast. As a result, they have to find a way to moralize mental illness and make it the fault of the sufferer. That way, they can avoid the judgmental and questioning eye that will wonder if such a fate will befall another rich, white man at any point soon.

Republicans ignoring the real and true nature of mental health and mental illness in this country is the right-wing version of YOLO philosophy. If you're not suffering from mental illness, you have no reason to care about anyone that does if you are a Republican. Just keep doing what you do. Make that money, pollute that lake, and jack up that stock price. After all, you only live once. Hopefully if you happen to fall victim to some sort of mental illness, you'll have enough money to deal with it privately and away from the inquiring rich, white men who wonder if you'll have what it takes to run the company when you return from your "sabbatical". Privilege really does pay off, especially when it's unearned.

The reality is that mental illness, particularly the stigma around it, destroys lives and can result in a tremendous amount of pain and torment for the sufferers and their families. There is a way to alleviate this problem, and it's really quite simple: provide state resources for mental health treatment. This country used to pour bucketloads of money into mental health treatment centers before Republican administrations worked day and night to defund them. Without those centers, mentally ill people were driven out into the streets to increase the homeless population and make it so that potentially productive people would be forced into lives of extreme poverty, violence, and pain. These seemingly simple policy decisions cause generational damage, and Republicans are directly responsible for causing it.

See, the Republican chess game on this issue is actually quite genius. A great deal of evil is incredibly intelligently crafted, and the conservative stance on mental health is a great example. Two crucial points of the Republican platform are used to keep people with mental health issues from getting treatment and therefore bettering their chances of ascending the social ladder. The first is their continued insistence on decreasing public spending at all costs. Keep in mind that this stance is designed to protect rich, white men from paying their fair share in taxes to support collective services that benefit everyone in society. By demanding that we decrease government spending and enacting policies that do just that whenever Republican administrations enter office, public spending on mental health is negatively affected. This leads to droves of mentally ill people becoming homeless. That checks box one of two on the Republican List of Evil.

But then, they up the ante even further. Once these people have been cast into poverty so that rich, white men won't have to pay another tax dollar to support their care, the Republican narrative of personal responsibility kicks in. To them, mentally ill people living on the streets should pull themselves up by their own bootstraps, get a job, and contribute to society. Meanwhile, the only reason that these people are on the streets in the first place is because Republicans took away the treatment centers that offered them the only real chance they had to get better and become more productive members of American society. With this, the Republican two-step is complete. They vote to take away the social safety net that keeps people from falling through the cracks, and then they blame people for having fallen through the cracks. If they don't pull themselves out of the cracks, somehow it's their fault. It's masterful evil.

The real reason that Republicans take these positions on mental health is that the most deleterious consequences of mental illness generally do not befall rich, white men. It is true that mental illness can affect everyone. But a bout of clinical depression can mean the difference between going to work and accruing the absence that results in termination for a working poor person who is living on the margins of society. If you work in a traditional white collar job, chances are your hours are far more flexible and you have the opportunity and resources to make the necessary appointments you need to address your individual circumstances. You can afford doctor's visits, you can afford medication, and you can afford to take time off work to take care of what you need to take care of. If you're a rich, white man, you don't need society's help to take care of your mental health. But the rest of us do. Luckily for Republicans, their mandate does not call for caring about anyone other than rich, white men.

This is evil, through and through. Republicans blatantly ignore a phenomenon that cuts across all socioeconomic strata and lean heavily on their privilege to carry them through the forest of their own hypocrisy. They know that staunch members of their own party will be felled by their own brain chemicals, but they depend on their own money and resources to get them out of it. But millions of Americans do not have the financial or social ability to adequately treat and cope with mental illness. Republicans throw them to the wolves and blame them for being eaten. This is all, keep in mind, to ensure the rich white men will have the ability to prosper without any interference from those pesky poor people and people of color. Mental illness may not discriminate by color of skin, but its effects certainly discriminate by socioeconomic status. Luckily, rich, white men can alter the landscape of discrimination. They can buy their way out of anything negative truly affecting them the way that it would affect a poor person or a person of color. Republicans certainly have the right to pay for their own treatment and make it so that mental illness has a minimal effect on their lives. But to deny public funding for mental health treatment and then blame sufferers for not picking themselves up and dusting themselves off is truly evil, and it deserves to be treated as such.

21

OPIOID CRISIS

America has been besieged by numerous public health crises throughout its relatively short history. These include the HIV/AIDS epidemic, the crack epidemic, and the polio epidemic, among many others. However, one of the most easily identifiable health crises in recent years is the opioid crisis that has taken a stranglehold in cities all across this country. There is no need to detail statistics here. The public perception and experience of the crisis speaks for itself. There are far more developed and nuanced sources that can lay out the statistics in greater detail than I have the time or ability to do here. But I think we can all agree that the opioid epidemic is just that: a crisis of opioid use that results in tragic addiction and deaths that damage far too many families in this country.

Let's walk through a typical fact pattern that has come to define the opioid crisis, particularly in the last few years. A young man suffers an injury and has to be taken to the hospital. Let's assume it's a back injury from playing football in the backyard. The doctor tells the young man that the injury does not require surgery, but that it will take some time to work itself out. The man tells the doctor that he won't be able to work at his full potential with the current state of the injury. No worry. That's why God invented painkillers. The doctor prescribes painkillers and he goes on his way. The injury improves a bit over the next week, but not enough so that the young man can work unimpeded without painkillers. The doctor gives him a refill and he takes it according to instructions. By this time, the young man is either very close to becoming addicted to the strong opioids coursing through his veins day after day, or he has actually finished the journey to full addiction. As time goes on, the doctor becomes more reluctant to provide refills. Eventually the doctor refuses to provide any further refills and leaves the young man to fend for himself, addicted to opioids and possibly still suffering from the original injury.

Dejected and in the throes of addiction, the young man is forced to find relief from unsavory sources. He may go out and score the same pills on the street. But, as these things often go, the addiction demands more and more from him. He has to take a handful of pills just to get to the same place that one pill got him weeks or months earlier. His default mental state is a place of darkness where it was once a neutral or positive place before the first pill hit his stomach. In order to get back to normal, his brain cells demand more and more of him just to get by. Eventually, he will need something more than just pills to get to a pain-free state. Even taking a handful of pills feels just as painful as the original injury. He needs so much more just for pain relief. The dopesickness rages and the sources of medication become less and less legal. He thinks that maybe he'll just try heroin. His parents always cautioned him never to touch the stuff, but he thinks he will literally be crippled with pain if he doesn't do something, anything to make it go away.

So he goes out and buys heroin from some shady guy in a back alley. He quickly becomes addicted to the stuff, far quicker than he got addicted to the pills in the first place. At this point, his family realizes that he really has a problem. The man has stopped showing up for work entirely. He is out at all hours and is asking his friends and family for money that, unbeknownst to them, is going to support his habit. He promises he'll pay them back but never does. Eventually, his boss gets fed up and fires him. His girlfriend gets fed up and leaves him. His family gets fed up and cuts off contact. The man is left broke and destitute, still going out every night to score. Eventually the drug overwhelms his fragile system and he winds up overdosing in the gas station bathroom he found to shoot up in. One more life is tragically snuffed out by the opioid epidemic, and it can all be traced back to those prescriptions from the foolhardy doctor.

The Republican stance on the opioid crisis will cause the above fact pattern to be replicated time and time again because it contemplates no real solution. Republicans, as always, pin a complex and nuanced social problem on a failing of personal responsibility. They want to preserve the system that they have in place to favor rich, white men. This necessitates blaming everyone else for their own problems while eliminating guilt for the rich, white men who often perpetuate and allow those problems to exist on a large scale in our country. It's important to look at the two ways that the Republican agenda works with respect to the opioid crisis: (1) keeping poor people and people of color down by blaming them for their own addictions and (2) protecting the rich, white men who benefit from the continuation of the opioid crisis.

First, addiction is a complex and heavily debated subject. In any event, it's clear that addiction exists in a space that is somewhat outside the realm of voluntary choice. One can choose to take a substance, but one generally does not choose to become addicted to it. I do not need to cite statistics for this to make sense. If you could be totally in control of your behavior, you could never get addicted to anything. You could simply choose to stop using a substance and never use it again. Addiction would not be a phenomenon, and no one would ever experience it. As a result, addiction is not something that can be blamed solely on one's choice. But Republicans want to blame all addicts for their addictions. Addiction is a moral flaw in the Republican framework, rather than a disease to be treated. This is convenient for Republicans, because it allows them to put all the poor addicts and people of color who are addicted to drugs into one basket and cast them aside without a second thought.

In their mind, it's all their fault and nothing needs to be done. If they want to get better, it's up to them. If they succumb to the addiction, that's on them. But nothing could be further from the truth. This is shown by the sheer number of rich, white men who have had to enter rehab programs in order to kick their own addictions. It's almost an archetype to show the rich businessman who becomes addicted to cocaine and has to take a "sabbatical" in order to recover. If the Republican narrative were correct, they would not have to enter rehab. They could just choose to get better. But most poor people and people of color in this country can't afford rehab programs, so it's easy to chalk their continuing addictions up to moral failing. Republicans get what they want fairly easily. Addiction kills poor people and people of color, and they can be easily blamed for their own deaths. The poor people and brown people are gone and Republicans get to continue on living without blinking an eye. The Republican world keeps spinning.

As if the prospect of poor people and brown people dying without a perceived need to take action were not tantalizing enough, the Republican stance on the opioid crisis has the added benefit of protecting the rich, white men behind the crisis. There are two groups of people, predominantly rich white men, who stand to benefit from the continuation of the opioid crisis. These are doctors and executives of pharmaceutical companies. This is not to say that all doctors are bad people. But it's clear that doctors should probably not be prescribing as many opioids as they are. Some of them should even probably be held civilly or criminally liable for overprescribing. Doing this threatens a profession traditionally dominated by rich, white men. Republicans have never stood for this sort of threat, and they never will. Perhaps more directly, pharmaceutical companies are controlled almost exclusively by rich, white men.

Republicans will never allow these men to be scorned when poor people and brown people can take the brunt of the blame. They would rather just live to see another day while life after life falls to the addictive scourge of opioids. The narrative is all too convenient. It is almost, itself, addictive. But you have the option of electing officials who will help to solve this problem. Government has the ability to regulate opioid prescription and make it so that only people who need these drugs will be able to get them. We place those people in power. Voice your values at the polls and don't allow more lives to be cut down in their prime. Republicans certainly will if you let them.

22

AMERICAN IMPERIALISM

America has established itself as a powerful force throughout the world, inserting itself into global politics as well as the political issues that would at a different time be considered purely local. Between the number of territories that have been taken on as American affiliates or states and our continued military presence throughout the world, it's hard to argue that the United States is anything other than an empire. In an age where the consequences of imperialism and colonialism are better understood than ever, nations are moving away from this model and their former ward nations are allowed to define and govern themselves. However, America is one of relatively few countries that is clinging tight to its imperialist ways, and Republicans are largely to blame.

There's no reason to go into the numerous examples of American imperialism here, because one only needs to look at places like Puerto Rico and American Samoa to see what our influence and violence is capable of. Rather, it's important to look at how the continuation of the American imperialist experiment is largely the fault of Republicans and the values they espouse. Remember, the Republican platform is at its core based on favoring rich, white men and keeping everyone else down. Imperialism achieves both of these aims particularly well, while also unleashing unspeakable evil on those lands unfortunate enough to be infected by our ravenous greed and lust for power.

The vast majority of places that America has co-opted over the last centuries were made up of largely poor, brown people when Americans arrived. Republicans have continued this trend by insisting on useless wars that ultimately result in permanent American presence in the theater of combat. Remember when we had an exit plan for Afghanistan? Don't be surprised if Republicans persist in that conflict long enough to collect every drop of oil available in the Middle East. Meanwhile, people are dying and governmental vacuums are giving rise to unspeakable violence and acts of terror. This is the new Manifest Destiny. Let's call it Republican Destiny.

Much like Manifest Destiny, Republican Destiny foists the values of the rich, white man upon the residents of foreign countries without their consent through threats of violence and military conflict. Unlike Manifest Destiny, Republican Destiny is attained through justifications like the War on Terror and general ramblings about national security. Make no mistake, the underlying desires and outcomes are the same. Republicans want the entire world to be just like America. To the extent that anything is non-American, which is really to say non-rich or non-white, it is wrong according to the Republican worldview. Conservatives stand ready to cure this illness at all costs, even if it means shedding the blood of men, women, and children in other countries to get the job done.

If you believe that America has spread itself too thin around the world, demand that we stop expanding military bases in other countries. We have no business meddling in their affairs. National security begins and ends at home, and we don't need to infringe on local customs and politics in order to ensure the safety of our own citizens. Republicans are the ones that insist on greater military spending in order to achieve this aim. We all know their ultimate goal. They want to control the world, expand capitalism to make rich white men richer, and use the opportunity to put a firm boot on the neck of the poor brown people that already live in other parts of the globe. It's all incredibly convenient for them.

Republicans vote for wars. They will continue to vote for wars, always and forever. They want to oppress people all across the world and spread their doctrine to anyone who will listen. Upon realizing that they don't fit into the doctrine, the unwitting victims will be promptly oppressed and sacrificed if necessary. The Republican world keeps turning. Vote these people out of power. Don't let them use your tax dollars to keep constructing this perverse Rube Goldberg device. Tell them that you've had enough. Otherwise, there's no telling just how far they'll go. Indeed, they might even pick a fight that we can't win. By then it will be too late.

23

THE SUPREME COURT

The American judicial system has become increasingly politically polarized over time. What was once intended to be a vehicle for upholding the law, reviewing new laws for constitutionality, and ensuring justice became a means for political parties to air their grievances and fight for their own aims. The problem has only gotten worse with respect to the Supreme Court of the United States. Entire presidential campaigns are now optimized for the purpose of placing justices on the Supreme Court. In fact, it appears now that Republicans have gotten their way. In electing Donald Trump, arguably the worst candidate to run and the worst president to be elected, they have likely secured the ability to set the course of the Court for the next several decades.

For better or worse, the Supreme Court has been the crucible in which several of our most crucial rights have been forged and recognized. These include the right of a woman to obtain an abortion, the right of same-sex couples to marry, and the right of Americans to have access to affordable health care. All of these public goods have had to fight the Republican establishment before the highest court in the land. Luckily, they all survived...for now. Others, like the right of a gay couple to purchase a cake without discrimination, were not so lucky.

But Republicans have changed the game. Where once the lawyers of Republican administrations served as the final boss in the comical video game that is human rights in America, Republicans are now turning the Court itself into the final boss. The party will now be judge, jury, and executioner as long as a Republican president and Congress are in power. This is exactly what they wanted all along. Now they can do anything they want to further the interests of rich, white men and oppress minorities and people of color with impunity. Expect the judicial landscape to fully transform into a godless wasteland where no one can hope to go for justice. The blindfold of justice will be ripped off and placed over the eyes of the American people while Lady Justice herself accepts a bribe for throwing another poor black man in prison.

Every Republican effort before the Supreme Court has been to achieve the same goals they seek to achieve in every other facet of political life in America. We have no reason to be surprised. They argued against abortion rights because they want to force women to carry unwanted pregnancy to term. They argued against same-sex marriage because they want to keep gay people from being happy and enjoying lives of fulfillment. They argued against affirmative action programs because they wanted to maintain their stranglehold over higher education. It's a veil, albeit a thin one. Conservative justices will roll back all of this progress and more with several strokes of the pen. The decisions may seem well-reasoned, but they will all undoubtedly favor rich, white men and work against women, minorities, and poor people.

The judiciary was always intended to be neutral. The letter and intent of the law were meant to govern, and it was clear to all with a brain that the constitution is a living document that is meant to adapt to changing times and social climates. But Republicans pushed the ideas of strict constructionism and originalism in order to make sure that the constitution would be interpreted in line with the intent of the Founders. Why do you think this is? Does anyone honestly think that the Founders had some unique wisdom that is not accessible to today's citizenry? It should be abundantly clear that Republicans want to maintain the Founders' vision because the Founders were some of the most vocal proponents of the rights and prosperity of rich, white men. After all, they were rich, white men who left a monarchy in order to avoid what they viewed as oppressive taxation. They literally founded a new country just to keep more of their money. Any time you doubt the true intentions of modern-day Republicans, remember what the Founders of this country did. They did all this, mind you, while fighting for the right to own black people.

The Supreme Court upheld these aims for most of its history, holding that black people could be viewed as property by the states, that racial segregation was perfectly legal, and that Japanese people could be legally interned without due process in a time of war. It was only in the latter half of the twentieth century that the Court woke up and realized what the constitution actually dictated in these situations. It took us over a half-century to actually attain meaningful social progress, and Republican administrations threaten to set the clock back in a fraction of that time. Now that Trump has the opportunity to replace sitting justices that have passed away or retired, it is only a matter of time before this nightmare becomes a reality.

Think about the sorts of rights you take for granted now. If you are a woman, you have the right to obtain an abortion if you so choose. Black people and white people can eat in the same restaurants. Health insurance companies can no longer discriminate against you for "preexisting conditions". Expect some, if not all, of these things to go away as soon as a Republican majority hits the bench. Their oppressive ideology will soon become the law of the land once again, and there's very little we can do about it.

Our only hope is to change the tide of public opinion to make such holdings virtually unenforceable. If clerks resolve to keep issuing marriage certificates to same-sex couples and make their intentions known, it's possible that the Court won't overturn its same-sex marriage decision at all. The Supreme Court should be neither a political branch nor an institution that responds to public pressure, but we know that it is both. This is our only hope to fight for the rights we have been fortunate enough to enjoy in recent years. If we don't fight back now, this country will return to being one nation, under God, for the white man, with liberty and justice for no one else.

24

MIDDLE AMERICA

Republicans keep winning elections despite losing the popular vote. This is due, of course, to the existence of the Electoral College. But in order for the College to hand Republicans these victories, there must be a large swath of the country that tends to vote Republican. Most liberal people live on either the East or West coast of the United States. That, of course, leaves all the land between the two coasts.

They're hiding in plain sight, friends. Republicans. Republicans everywhere. We callously dismiss these areas as "flyover states" and "farm country" without taking time to understand what they really are. This is where the Republican base lives. These are the white people who have a particular set of values that do not harmonize with progressive thought. Of course, this is not true of every person who lives in Middle America. But the Republican base does live here, and it's important to examine exactly the kinds of people they are.

These are the communities that have existed for hundreds of years and have very little turnover or diversity. Advocating for the party that favors rich, white men is easy for them. They hold their religion close and spurn anything that is different. These are the neighborhoods that flee as soon as a black person moves into the neighborhood. While there are many good people who live here, most of whom are incredibly disillusioned by the constant boring repression that engulfs them, Middle America is also home to most of the worst people that this country has to call its own.

There is inherently something different about the culture of Middle America as a whole. While coastal communities were shaped by immigrants and the influx of minorities seeking to escape the oppressive nature of the South, Middle America has largely remained dull and white. While the freight train of whiteness was somewhat slowed by increases in diversity on the coasts, it has barreled on unimpeded in Middle America. Whiteness is still highly prized in these areas. It's uncommon for people to marry outside their race, and many residents have never met a gay person or a lesbian. Most of what we consider to be progress is wholly foreign to these areas of the country. In times past, I would almost be inclined to argue that it was not their fault. It's difficult to blame people for not being exposed to people or concepts that just do not exist in their area. But in the age of the internet and rapid exchanges of information, it's virtually inexcusable to lack the level of exposure to diverse viewpoints that result in a progressive mindset.

This is why Middle America continues to be a despondent place, devoid of culture and meaningful social progress. They keep voting for politicians who actively work against their best interests. People in these communities are largely obsessed with the prosperity of the industries that have historically supported them. However, the rise of automation and outsourcing has left many of these areas without a reliable industry, and economic despair has quickly followed. Middle America has thus become quite easy for Republicans to manipulate. All they have to do is go there, blame minorities and immigrants for taking their jobs, promise to bring the industries back, and leave with a majority of their vote.

Meanwhile, when these Republican candidates are elected, they'll keep advocated for the interests of rich, white men as they always have. Rich, white men generally do not live in Middle America. They live on the coasts because they value the culture and talent pools that exist there. Quite frankly, it's just more fun to live on the coasts. Republicans in Middle America are left holding the bag. They lose the industries that they were destined to lose anyway, and the rich politicians and businessmen make off with their continued political support. It's a win-lose situation.

This all raises the question: Why would Middle Americans continue to support Republicans if it's obvious that Republicans only care about rich, white men? After all, most of the people living in Middle America are either middle or lower class, even though most of them are white. The answer is that most white people in these areas view themselves as people who will be rich one day. In their mind, they are voting in their own self-interest because they want the laws to favor rich, white men by the time they become rich, white men. After all, we're talking about small business owners, career laborers, cubicle dwellers, and people who play the lottery planning to win. White Middle Americans view wealth as the province of white men, and they plan to claim their share sooner rather than later. As a result, they'd prefer the political and legal atmosphere to be favorable once they arrive.

These are largely not great people we're talking about here. Even if they are not abject and overt racists, they have benefited from the social and legal structures that have favored white people for this country's entire history. This is not a problem for individuals, per se, if they check their privilege and strive to better society through pushes for diversity and inclusion. But that's not what these people do. Instead, they stay to themselves and blame minorities for the fact that they're not rich. These are the people who blame illegal immigration for the fact that they are unemployed. Meanwhile, they harp on about the fact that liberals just need to grow up and get jobs. By and large, these are insufferable individuals. They have little to no exposure to life outside of their communities, and their exclusionary attitudes reflect that fact.

They're a perfect Republican base. They're also the reason that the Electoral College is a ridiculous institution that needs to be abolished. If we had a true democracy, elections would be won by the candidate that received the most votes, period. Instead, we have this asinine system that only exists to give disproportional representation to people living in Middle America. Why should your state dictate how much your vote counts? If most people settle on the coasts and have a certain way of looking at the world due to the culture of coastal cities, then the majority should govern. It's no secret that the Electoral College has worked almost exclusively for Republicans and against Democrats. You'll never hear a Republican advocate for the end of the Electoral College.

Middle America will always go Republican. These oblivious privileged people sit in their backyards, grill their hot dogs, drink their beer, and remain ignorant of the reality of the world around them. Anyone who is suffering from racial discrimination, gender-based violence, or income inequality has likely woven these concepts out of whole cloth and is using them to take blame off themselves. They pretend that there's no fire around them because they've locked themselves in a fireproof safe. There's not much that can be done, because people have the right to be who they are. But it's important to realize that kinds of people that go out and vote for Republicans. Keep that in mind when you're deciding whether your vote really matters.

25

HOMELAND SECURITY

America was once a nation that considered itself secure without needing to strip its citizenry of rights guaranteed to them under the constitution. Then 9/11 happened. Now, it seems that constitutional rights are disappearing with each new conservative-authored Supreme Court opinion and Republican-signed law. From increased warrantless searches to engaging in warfare abroad without congressional approval, America has taken incredibly brazen action in the name of national security. Where the government once needed to put forward some sort of justification for invading a country or narrowing the application of the Fourth Amendment's prohibition against warrantless searches and seizures, a different process is now in place. A Republican political now just utters the words "national security" and promptly earns carte blanche.

While all Americans were affected by the tragedies of 9/11, Republicans used it as an opportunity to expand the government's influence over the lives of American citizens and the political affairs of other countries. As you may recall from a discussion earlier in this book regarding American imperialism, Republicans will stop at nothing to ensure that the ways of the rich, white male American can be spread as far as possible. This boils down to a lust for pure, unadulterated power. But power is difficult to obtain, even with privilege, without a broader appeal to the general populace. The national security argument provided Republicans with just the ammunition they needed to continue their fight for affluence and whiteness.

Let's take a look at a few examples of the ways in which Republicans have used the notion of "national security" to effect patently wrong and evil outcomes. First is the expansion of the American military and its efforts. Second is the increased presence of law enforcement officials running frivolous missions in certain localities. Third is the increasingly clandestine operations that the federal government engages in generally. Fourth is the increase in federal government spying efforts in the name of reducing the risk of terrorism. There are far more than four manifestations of national security run amok. But an exhaustive discussion of all the remaining issues is work better done by another author in another volume dedicated to the task. Let's address each of these four examples one by one.

The American military has been a Republican pet project for several decades. It has become the primary tool for increasing American influence and dominance around the globe. Naturally, Republicans are attracted to this potential like the moth to the flame. But Republicans could not stop with the power of the military at the time that they took an interest. No, it had to grow bigger and stronger. This took money to accomplish. Unlike most Republican stances, the fetishization of the military celebrated an increase in the use of tax dollars to increase a concrete government expenditure. Even though these tax dollars came from rich, white men (as well as the rest of us), Republicans considered the whole endeavor to be worth it. Expanding the influence of America and its associated wealth and whiteness was just that important.

Unfortunately, 9/11 handed Republicans the opportunity they craved. It allowed them to implement an exponential increase in military spending, as well as an associated increase in government contracts with private weapons and technology developers. This was used to wage conflicts that were started without the consent of

Congress. These fruits of those conflicts rage on as of this writing. Our troops have been dragged into conflicts that have led them to their death, all for the sake of having another American toe dipped in the broader global pool. Was it worth it, Republicans? Were the military bases in numerous sovereign countries not enough? You just had to have dead troops on top of it all. Will anything ever be enough?

With increased military conflicts come inevitable externalities beyond the loss of American troops. These include, at the very least, the killing of tens of thousands of foreign citizens, destabilization of foreign governments without a developed plan of succession, and disturbing the global political landscape. Without a proximate threat to the American people, it is incredibly difficult to justify these offensive maneuvers. But there is an related and equally severe consequence to the expansion of the American military. Our government and armed forces seem to inevitably get drawn into committing war crimes and crimes against humanity. Specifically, we have become the kind of people that torture citizens of foreign countries in the name of a national cause. We dedicate taxpayer money to "enhanced interrogation" with little regard paid to the promises we made under myriad international agreements. Our philosophy has become to torture first and ask questions later. This is not who we are as a people, and we need to do better. Elect politicians who will vow not to increase the size or power of our military without an appropriate reason for doing so. Specifically, refuse to vote for Republicans and do everything you can to keep the people in your life from voting for Republicans. It could literally mean life or death for our troops.

While Republicans have the military doing their bidding abroad, they have law enforcement agencies at their fingertips on American soil. The military fulfills the Republican aim of spreading their version of American-ness around the world. But the police carry out their marching orders by attempting to correct every instance of nonconformity. If it falls outside the realm of richness, whiteness, and maleness, it is deeply flawed according to the Republican worldview. The police can patrol certain areas disproportionately, arrest with near impunity, and search property with only the fear that the evidence they find may not be able to be used in a court of law. These are quite unique powers to wield, and Republicans seem well-positioned to handle them. After all, they have become masters of oppression and fascistic suppression of any sort of culture or expression that runs contrary to their own.

If you need an example of how Republicans use their control over the police to further their aims of favoring rich, white men and oppressing poor people and people of color, just look at the rash of police killings of unarmed black men over the last few years. A detailed discussion of these deplorable acts would require its own book. But one look at the evening news at some point in the last five years shows that the police have a huge problem with black people. Between broken windows policing and the disproportionate arrest, conviction, and sentencing of black people for nonviolent drug offenses, the police have struggled to hide their discontent. But Republicans have implemented a great deal of the policy that has led to these heinous policing trends. Ducking behind an ill-fitting veil of being "tough on crime", Republicans have made it abundantly clear that they want the police to target anyone who is not a rich, white male.

They've succeeded with flying colors. Think of the rich, white kid I described earlier who was caught for smoking marijuana. Do you ever picture that kid going to prison for their crime? Of course not. Police have been trained not to treat rich, white young people like this. Now picture the same joint between the fingers of the poor, black kid I described earlier. You know you would be surprised if that kid didn't end up at least in the back of the police cruiser if not in a jail cell. When that kid grows up and gets into an argument with the wrong police officer, he's incredibly likely to wind up being shot and killed. Keep in mind, this is the group of people who claim to only want to "protect and serve". These actions on the part of police departments and individual officers undoubtedly contribute to white privilege in America. If you believe that having no reasonable fear of being shot by the police due to the color of your skin is not privilege, I have some swamp land to sell you. Republicans get their wish yet again.

As if local law enforcement overreach were not enough for Republicans, federal law enforcement agencies have done just as much if not more to attain Republican aims. To further the interests of white men, Republican administrations developed and expanded Immigration and Customs Enforcement ("ICE" for short) in order to reign in the fictional scourge of illegal immigration. Instead of fulfilling its mandate to patrol the border and protect America from any criminals seeking to use the border as a means to gain access to their targets, ICE has dedicated itself to separating children from their families and tearing apart longstanding immigrant communities in the name of national security interests. Policymakers conjured up half-brained rationales for increasing "enforcement" of our immigration laws and allowed ICE to go on a series of raids that would make even Ronald Reagan blush. Tax dollars follow these sinister agents to their raids and fund an exercise in destroying communities, culture, and social ties. Keep telling yourself that Republicans only care about enforcing the law. It's no coincidence that these efforts are targeted almost exclusively at Latino/a individuals. People cross the Canadian border illegally, too. But you won't see crackdowns on those immigrants, because they have the skin color that Republicans love.

Couple these atrocities with the growth in agencies like the DEA, whose supposed aim is to curb drug crime in the United States. Instead, they conduct raids on primarily minority communities under the guise of being tough on crime, and throw scores of black and brown people in prison for nonviolent offenses. Is the continuation of this kind of law enforcement what you really want to vote for on Election Day? Republicans don't support these measures out of the goodness of their hearts. There's something in it for them: namely, the oppression of anyone who is not a rich, white male.

The government activities that we hear about in the media are merely the tip of the iceberg. Most government efforts take place in secret, and impact global politics in a way that generates the least amount of buzz possible. From CIA black sites to the FBI's surveillance of Dr. Martin Luther King, Jr., we can easily see that the government does not tell us nearly everything it does. Considering that the government is supposed to be accountable to the people, it's important to ask why the government needs to keep so much from us. A certain amount of secrecy is understandable. America's enemies would benefit greatly from the disclosure of a great deal of our classified information. However, tracking and undermining civil rights leaders is hardly a national security concern. Republicans have vocally supported efforts to increase the ability of the government to operate in secret for quite some time now. They have a vested interest in cultivating and maintaining this kind of power. It comes in handy when your overall aim is to subjugate minorities and people of lesser means.

By retaining the ability to run investigations, gather intelligence, and conduct covert operations on American citizens, Republicans have locked in virtually plenary authority over anyone that disagrees with them. These unconstitutional measures are a direct line between Republicans and maintaining the power of rich, white men in this country. The odd part is that Republicans claim to be the party of small government. Republicans could not be further from being accurately called the party of small government. They actually want a government made up of just enough rich, white men to swallow and subjugate the rest of the country. Don't let them fool you.

This brings us to the issue of government surveillance generally. Between programs like those authorized by the PATRIOT Act and FISA and institutions like the NSA that are dedicated to gathering our information for God knows what ultimate use, we have every reason to be deeply concerned. Much like the DEA and ICE, these are institutions and programs largely spearheaded by Republicans. The so-called "War on Terror" ushered in large swaths of additional surveillance authorizations and programs in rapid succession. But completely preventing terror attacks is not only statistically improbable, it's very likely not the reason that these institutions were devised in the first place. Republicans are so obsessed with keeping themselves in power that they have become dedicated to knowing everything there is to know about everyone else. They have become paranoid about any and everything that threatens their death grip on authority. As a result, they concocted a vain ruse to dupe the American citizenry into thinking that further surveillance was necessary to further national security interests.

Think for just a second about whom these additional surveillance programs have typically targeted. The most common victims of this intrusion are Muslims and other brown people. The government has sold the American people a story regarding Islam and terror, claiming that the two are somehow inextricably related. They've conveniently ignored the narrative about the undeniable relationship between whiteness and oppression of minorities. But then again, they hope that you never think critically about that. As long as they can spy on Muslims without fear of unrest or political harm, they're going to do it. Rich, white men in government have tricked Americans into thinking that additional surveillance is good and that terrorist attacks would be imminent without these disgusting programs. With that fear in hand, they can virtually get away with anything.

Their influence and directives extend into virtually every aspect of our lives. How can we feel safe online, talking to our loved ones on the phone, or even having a conversation in public when we know that someone might be listening? If you take even a cursory look at news stories concerning government surveillance, you should be shocked at what you see. This information gathering campaign strengthens the government's fight against crime, at least in poor and minority communities. White communities somehow get off a little bit easier. It doesn't take much to figure out why that is.

Republicans have made it so that the government can spy on whomever they want without fear of repercussion. National security cannot mean spying on every potential threat, no matter how remote. In what sense of the word is our nation supposed to feel "secure" in such a system? Our republic feels more and more fractured every day. This is due in no small part to the fact that we have more access to the lives of our fellow citizens. With social media and general over-sharing, we cannot help but become wary and envious of our neighbors. If voluntary disclosure of this information has led to this disastrous outcome, what do you think will happen to the relationship between Americans and our government? I cannot think of a time during which we as Americans have trusted our government less. This is a powerful entity devised and restricted by the constitution, charged with the task of ensuring the collective safety and welfare of the American people. Yet it cannot serve its function, and it has been unable to do so for quite some time. Republicans are to blame for this fracturing.

America is supposed to be a fantastic union and a grand experiment in democracy and constitutional governance. But by injecting government into the most minute daily transactions and interactions between human beings, Republicans have turned us all against each other, united in despising the government. This is all to further the interests of rich, white men and to oppress everyone else. What better way is there to achieve this aim than to make everyone hate each other? To Republicans, the ends justify the means. As long as their share prices remain high, their bank account balances soar, and they remain free of police suspicion, they're happy to foist any amount of discomfort upon poor people and people of color. This is true even if they have to manufacture a story to convince us that our country is constantly under threat. They tell us our national security is on the brink of failure, and that spying on our citizens is the only way to keep our great country together. But in the end, they seek to divide us all and unite themselves as they always do.

26

REPUBLICAN CULTURE

Culture informs politics and politics informs culture. It's a dance that communities of all sizes engage in until a happy medium of some sort is ultimately reached. However, it always seems to be the case that one side generally leans toward culture informing politics while the other leans toward politics informing culture. Sometimes these sides switch, usually in response to some some sociocultural event that is greater than both of them.

Over the last few decades, liberal politics have informed liberal culture. The general favor of inclusiveness, economic equality, and overall tolerance lends itself well to creative endeavors. This is why almost every artist worthy of any respect is some flavor of liberal. You don't see many prominent conservative artists. If you do, they're very often hacks or somehow legitimately disingenuous. Some of them are trying to make a statement by working in counterculture. You'll find that their actual beliefs are more liberal than they claim. Music, visual art, television, movies, you name it, are all very heavily informed by liberal politics. Try coming out as a conservative in Hollywood. You'll get the negative reaction you so dearly deserve.

But Republicans have primarily had their politics informed by their culture. This might explain why Republican politics are so narrow, thin, and shallow. Liberalism means so many things to so many different people. It takes on as many shades as are reflected in the racial demographics of liberals. But Republican culture takes on one shade, just like Republicans themselves. That culture is the sort of boring, pasty white of a generic apartment wall. Their rainbow looks like rice, pasta, and white bread all on a white ceramic plate. There's some difference between those things, but not really. It's all still white. Republican politics have become equally bland as a result.

They really only care about preserving America for the betterment of white people. Republicans view themselves as the successors of warriors fighting the good fight of white supremacy. It's no longer acceptable to openly carry that mantle, but the sentiment has infected Republican culture, perhaps irredeemably so. The effect is so deep that it persists despite its subtlety. Most Republicans are hardly aware, if they are aware at all, of the historical roots that affect their culture and, in turn, define their politics.

Think about a typical Republican community for a minute. Place yourself in the Middle America discussed earlier in this book. What do you see? Do you see the vibrant cityscape of a New York City or Los Angeles? Do you see the veritable rainbow of skin tones scattered up and down the city streets, each carrying with it a unique story and history? Do you see the art and culture dripping from the skyscrapers and bathing the city in a warm and welcoming atmosphere? With very few exceptions, it's overwhelmingly likely that you don't. You likely see a slow way of living, defined by routine, awash in uniformity. People go to school from the time they are young children, do the same things as their friends (who all look exactly like them), graduate, go to the local college, get a job in one of a few local industries, marry someone they've known since kindergarten, have children before the age of 24, grow to resent everything in their lives, commit themselves to maintaining social norms as payback for their misery, grow old, and die without having seriously questioned the world around them. Their lives seem to run on as long as that last sentence.

Their existence lacks panache, heat, and verve. Mustard is spicy to these people. Comfort in these communities breeds fear of the unknown. Bigotry and hatred of those who are different naturally follows in quick succession. A black family moves to the neighborhood, and everyone is up in arms. If everyone is up in arms, than a given person must be up in arms too. Going against the grain does not bode well for a community that is based entirely on conformity. To get a job, to earn a promotion, and to advance generally in these areas requires the sort of good ol' boy attitude and fear of change that, when aggregated, becomes privilege and general whiteness. Multiply this paradigm by the number of these communities to be found in Middle America, and you have the Republican base.

Republican politics is just an extension of this culture. The reason that Republicans call themselves "conservatives" is that they want to conserve a particular way of life. The times they long for are what we would call the days of old. There was a time when most of America fit into the Middle American White Republican mold. They want to go back there. To them, the influx of minorities and their culture changed that way of life into something they no longer recognize. Combine that with a perverse desire to horde resources and wealth, and you get the current Republican platform, easily boiled down into a desire to favor rich, white men.

Republican culture is defined in negative terms, or more specifically, what they don't want to see in this country. For this reason, there's next to no focus on what they do want to see in this country. All they know for sure is that they want to see the prosperity of white people. Everything else is a negative. They don't want to see minorities, poor people, prosperous women, or people with different religious beliefs. When you push everyone else out of your life, all you have is yourself. Unlike liberals who have the music of black people, the food of Asian cultures, and the literature of the great Latin@ authors, Republicans only have whiteness. Republican culture is unappealing precisely because it lacks diversity. Food is boring if you eat the same thing every day. They only have one cultural input, while liberals are discovering new ones every day.

Because Republican culture is so simple, it's incredibly easy to manipulate. As long as you play within the simple rules and structures discussed above, you can get almost anything you want. A reality TV show star can become president by using a particular series of tired words and ideas to secure millions and millions of votes. Meanwhile, liberals demand a great deal from their leaders. You have to prove that your ideas stand up to the bar of progress, wherever it may stand at that particular time. You have to be educated, articulate, and empathetic. To win as a Republican, you basically just have to be white and loud. This is why liberal culture will always triumph over Republican culture. If liberals keep succeeding in bringing about progress, the age to which Republicans long to return will fall further and further away in society's rear view mirror.

Perhaps the most beautiful part of Republican culture is the fact that most Republicans don't even understand what it is. Most of them don't even acknowledge the power of culture. They claim to just be living their lives, desirous of freedom from the twin fists of tyranny and oppression. Instead, their collective desire to maintain the norms of the past form the fingers that curl up and become those fists. One hand knows not what the other is doing, but they somehow manage to oppress everything else in tandem. It's all so simple, yet so poorly understood. Liberals, by contrast, are raised and developed knowing what culture is and how it affects the world. Knowing how and why culture changes and how it can be optimized does most of the work of fighting for tolerance all on its own. The labor is done in the background while liberals live their lives reaping the fruits of their own subconscious effort.

This is all done through the conscious and voracious consumption of knowledge. As knowledge increases, conservatism decreases. Republican high-schoolers who leave for liberal colleges come back liberals because they have actually learned something. Conservatives tell themselves that life is about living and surviving. But humanity is about so much more than that. Self-examination and the critical evaluation of society is crucial to the formation of well-adjusted and compassionate citizens. Republican culture lacks these things entirely. This is why most people living in that culture drift through life, vapidly moving from one preset norm to another, destined to be mentally handcuffed to their locale. These are the manual laborers who dreamed of nothing better. Manual labor can be entirely fulfilling as long as one knows one's full potential. That potential can be in living a full life replete with inquiry and knowledge. Republicans do not do this. Instead, they depend on creating and harvesting a crop of obedient drones dedicated to voting with the party line every couple of years.

People living in primarily Republican areas are not inherently dense or dull. We have seen numerous urban and evolved areas develop in what had previously been the middle of an intellectual nowhere. This all comes together with the help of knowledge and the dissemination of information. You would think that in the age of the internet, this goal would be easier than ever to attain. But there is at play here a unique combination of suppression of free thought and a cultural unwillingness to advance. One of these can be fixed and the other cannot. Unfortunately, one almost always results in the other. You can't fix cultural unwillingness to advance, but cultures can reinvent themselves. It's incredibly unlikely that most predominantly Republican communities can make this change. As a result, we should expect them to stay this way for the foreseeable future.

Imagine for a second what it is actually like to live in these sorts of locales. People call you gay for having any interest in cultures other than your own. Everyone in your town is white, inherently limiting your selection for a mate as you progress through life. Exoticism is shamed and any difference is a black mark on your societal record. You're expected to do what everyone else does. You go to work, come home, eat, and go to bed. You do all this for forty or fifty years, retire, and die. Is it any wonder that these people vote Republican? They don't know any other way. When social pressure mounts on you to keep things exactly the way they are, you're going to vote for the candidate who promises to do just that. That candidate assures you that all your problems are the fault of some brown person you never met, or that the liberals are getting in the way of being your best self.

You vote the way everyone else votes, and you tell yourself you've done something good.

This is what Republican culture is. It's inherently oppressive and repressive. It claims that beautiful flowers are weeds because they don't look like the rest of the plants in the garden. If we want to make change, we have to see issues through the lens of this disastrous set of beliefs. You would absolutely hate your life if you had to grow up in these communities. These people are not happy. They vote for Republican candidates because they feel like they have to. We can make real change if we engage with Republican culture rather than fighting it. Information is our best asset in trying to convince people to cross the aisle. These people are not necessarily dumb. There are just greater powers in place making sure that they don't learn. Educated people are liberal for a reason. We can't blame Republicans for everything, but we do have to be honest about where they come from. If not, we risk losing more elections to a backwards culture that denies progress and the legitimacy of all Americans.

27

FIGHTING BACK

The liberal way of life is under attack. Hate crimes are on the rise, racism is still prevalent in American society, and we are turning back the clock on decades of progress. Democrats keep on losing presidential elections, congressional seats, and state governorships. Every time we see election results that usher in another Republican, a small piece of the American dream dies yet another painful death. The futures of brown children take another hit and risk being further and further removed from true happiness and fulfillment.

It would be easy to sit here and say that combating rich, white male privilege would be sufficient to ensure that progress has an unimpeded path. But it isn't. We have to do so much more. That privilege has leached into the collective water supply that is our political discourse. Our country is taking a hard right turn, and liberals have to come together in a collective garrison and prepare to take a stand. Our division is our defeat. To the extent that we refuse to take collective action, we hand our country over to those who want to see the lives of women, poor people, and people of color commoditized and crushed under the wheels of unbridled capitalism. Republicans have formed a reliable bloc for many decades. They can count on their vote. Liberals can't even count on voters to show up to the polls. We have to do better.

So how do we fight back? How do we take our country back from the heartless heathens who have found themselves in power? Our only option is to come together behind a common set of goals. We have to stand up for what we believe in. Moderation is no longer an option. If liberals remain moderate, there is a real risk of losing membership to the Republicans and bolstering their unearned position of power. We have to make a checklist and turn that set of beliefs into a set of marching orders. You're either with us or against us. I suspect that there are untold numbers of individuals who would fight for a unified liberal cause. The problem is that no one can really figure out what liberals stand for anymore.

Stop arguing over issues that have a clear liberal resolution. It's clear where we stand on single-payer universal health care. It's clear where we stand on the expansion of welfare programs. It's clear where we stand on the rapid expansion of military and police power. We no longer need to debate how far we are willing to go with these ideas. The concepts themselves are radical, and they are appealing. Let liberal leaders figure out the exact policies when they get into office. We just have to get them there. We can no longer afford to keep putting the cart before the horse. You can never even hope to implement these principles in government if you can't get good people there in the first place.

Blind loyalty is never good, but the liberal vote needs to become incredibly predictable if we hope to continue moving the freight train of progress forward. Right now, it is stalled on the tracks because a fat, orange-haired cow sat down in front of the train. We need to rebuild the blue wall and use it to keep Republicans from coming over and continuing to destroy civilization. We have to stop demanding anything from Democrats other than filling our revised liberal checklist. To the extent that a liberal has connections to big business or conservative-funded causes, they have to be chucked from the tent or change their ways. We can't afford to be the big, friendly tent that defined our tolerant and accepting positions in the past. We have to become aggressive about our tolerance and acceptance, as odd as that might sound.

Republicans are quick to point out that liberals are not actually all that tolerant because liberals don't tolerate Republicans particularly well. This is, of course, because Republicans are not particularly good at logical reasoning. In order to be tolerant, one necessarily needs to be intolerant of intolerance. If that confuses you, you probably did not do well in grade school math. A positive number can be the product of multiplying two positive numbers or multiplying two negative numbers. Tolerance times tolerance equals tolerance. Intolerance times intolerance also equals tolerance. It's only when you multiply tolerance by intolerance that you have a problem. Republicans tolerate intolerance. That's why they have so many problems. Liberals are consistent. Don't let Republicans tell you otherwise by using this nonsense argument.

But we have to hunker down and commit to the tolerant and accepting positions we have honed over the years. If a candidate has an issue with gay people, they're out. If they have an issue with brown people, they're out. If they have an issue with universal health care, they're out. These issues are no longer negotiable. They are, quite literally, matters of life and death. We have to think of them this way. We've become far too soft. Liberals have become so soft that the term "social justice warrior" is now almost exclusively used in jest. We have to be warriors, but we have to convince others that our causes are worth fighting for. Having large numbers of people shouting and clamoring for the same thing can convince people very quickly.

There are four core things liberals have to do in order to make sure that the results above can be firmly and quickly secured. First, we have to vote. Second, we have to develop a real platform that serves as a litmus test for everyone who claims to be a liberal. Third, we have to publicly and loudly call Republicans out on their hateful ways. Finally, we have to create and foster a culture that values people over money. These are not easy things to do. Some of them will take a lifetime, if not more. But it all has to start now. Republicans are not far from establishing unbreakable majorities in several major governmental institutions for the foreseeable future. Slowing the spread of their toxic ideology is possible, but it will require a great deal of work.

Liberals, you have to get off the couch and vote. The beautiful thing about liberalism is that it draws in all sorts. Most people are good people who want to use our collective societal resources to make a stable and well-funded set of social programs to care for those that need it. But the one downside of having such a diverse base is that you get some lazy people. It's okay. I don't pretend to know what's going on in everyone's lives, and I'm sure people have perfectly acceptable reasons for not voting. But Donald Trump's election raised the stakes so high that you can no longer afford not to vote. Your life, freedom, and values are all on the line. If you don't show up, the blood our our society is on your hands.

Voting needs to become one of the biggest priorities that liberals hold dear. Our turnout rates should be as close to a hundred percent as possible. Vote absentee if you need to and are allowed to do so in your circumstances. Make plans to be able to go and vote in person if you can't vote absentee. You would take the day off if your kid were sick, right? Take the day off to make sure that your kid will be able to survive illness or injury without bankrupting your entire household. There are very few good reasons for not voting. Being in a coma is one. I guess if you're actually being eaten by a bear on Election Day, we can give you a pass. Although, I must admit, I still wonder why you didn't go ahead and vote absentee if you knew you'd be in the woods on Election Day. We're at cultural and political war here, people. Every vote counts.

To make our increased voting efforts worth our while, we need to craft and implement the sort of liberal checklist I discussed a few minutes ago. Republicans have a dogma. If you go against the dogma, they'll strike your name from the proverbial rolls and leave you to wander by yourself in the political wilderness. Liberals have to become this cold and calculating if we're going to get anything done. Developing a backbone will do more to attract voters than anything liberals have done to date. This will also require rich and powerful liberals to deny funding to any candidate who does not meet the criteria. Money talks louder than almost any other force. It's how Republicans get things done. Let's take just one page out of their despicable playbook.

This will, of course, result in the overt rejection of otherwise palatable candidates. The loss of political viability for these would-be public officials is just going to be a cost of doing business. We have to show the world that we're serious about seeing our agenda through. These people have to become an example. Their political careers have to be sacrificed at the altar of progress and collective good. If they don't pass our litmus tests, they probably did not have our best interest at heart, anyway. It's better that we get them out of our political lives now, rather than having to clean up the mess they would inevitably cause later.

Like almost every major beneficial change, a great deal of pain has to come in order to bring about a greater good. We have to rip off the bandage, endure that suffering, and reveal the healed country and politics that will occupy the space where there once was gaping wound of discrimination and strife. You'll have to make difficult choices at the polls. This will likely require uniting around candidates that mainstream "liberals" will not want you to support. The Democratic Party will not nominate these people, because at the end of the day, radical change does not interest the party brass. Despite being leaps and bounds better than Republicans (as is literal garbage, by the way), Democrats have a long way to go to prove to us that they actually have the best interests of the American people in mind. Ending racism, ensuring guarantees of stable public assistance programs, and dismantling the culture that established a fast lane for rich, white men all have to be at the forefront of their platform. We have to make them do that by promising to vote against them if they don't. It may seem crass and it may seem boorish, but it is necessary.

The stakes are far too high here. We cannot continue to let Republicans make a mockery of our country in the name of making life easier for rich, white men. No longer should women, queer people, people of color, or anyone who is not a rich, white male suffer under the millstone of oppression that Republicans have carefully crafted for our demise. Unfortunately, they have severely limited our options. We have few tools to fight back. But we still have our vote. If we can collectivize our vote, we can make this country a place where everyone feels safe. This can be a land where everyone has an opportunity to create happiness and prosperity for themselves rather than the unfortunate need to slave away for a man who earns more in an hour than they will all year. It is time to reclaim at the polls what Republicans have stolen from us for generations: our dignity, our potential, and our hope.

If I sound desperate, it's because I am. We lost so much with Donald Trump's election. We fought for almost fifty years to take one step forward, and in one night Republicans set us two steps back. Ask the average person of color how they feel in this country now that Republicans have regained control of our government. I can guarantee you that the vast majority of us feel unsafe. We know that our lives can be ended by the bullet of an angry officer's gun, and that he will get off scot free because he "felt threatened" by what the color of our skin told him about the content of our character. This is no longer a matter of preference. This isn't even about politics anymore. This is life and death. Our lives and the lives of our children hang in the balance. That's why we need to get angrier. We have to get tougher. We have to stand up together and declare that we refuse to accept this new dystopia that has been foisted upon us. They need to know that the game is over.

Our situation is not hopeless, friends. Each of us has the potential to be a piece of the machinery that ultimately brings down the Republican establishment and takes their boots off our necks. Republicans are clearly not responsible for every single one of our problems, but odds are that if you have a major problem in your life that can't be directly tied to your own actions, Republicans are responsible for it in some way, shape or form. The student loan crisis, income inequality, gun violence, along with many other social problems that affect so many of our lives on a deeply personal level can be directly linked to Republican action or purposeful inaction. These problems are their fault, and it's about time that we started behaving that way.

This may be our last chance. Our vote may very well be the only thing left at our disposal to oust these despicable people from their positions of power. But we have to make this one count. We can't fracture our vote and disperse it to numerous candidates who satisfy different parts of our political goals. We have to put the work in up front. Any liberal candidate has to be ideal for the causes we actually believe in. They have to be someone that all of us can support. No longer can the left's vote be unreliable. Deep down, we all know that this is true, but now it is time to act on our knowledge.

As I come closer to the end of this rant, I have to note once more that we just don't have any time left to figure out or solidify our platform. We know right from wrong and we know what makes good policy and what doesn't. The next few years could determine the course of our country for the next century. Do we have what it takes to make sure that our children and grandchildren will live in a country with healthy infrastructure, reliable health care, and appropriate restrictions on assault weapons? I think we do. We've done this before. Our work over the last few decades has been impeccable and strong, but we still have more to do. When we take our last breath, we need to be able to look our kids in the eye and tell them that we did everything we could to make sure that they have a dependable future. But the journey to that statement begins now. Get out, go to the polls, and tell anyone who will listen what the left actually believes in and why. Explain exactly how Republicans have wrought havoc upon anyone who is not a rich, white man, and what can be done to fix it. If each of us does our part, we can be victorious. We can overcome oppression.

28

REPUBLICANS IN YOUR FAMILY

This could very well be the shortest chapter of this book. If you agree that Republicans are responsible for some of the most heinous and egregious sociopolitical conditions to ever occur in this country, it naturally leads to one question: What do I do about the people I care about who happen to be Republicans? Clearly people can't be expected to uproot their families and strike out on their own just because they happen to be related to Republicans. But the answer also can't be to just tolerate hateful and discriminatory viewpoints without resistance. That undermines our causes and everything we believe in. The answer is somewhat the opposite of the way that we fight back against Republican politicians. We have to disarm most of our loved ones with kindness and understanding. There are some who need tough love and intense discussion, but that won't be effective for most.

Political change can and will be won at the polls with the right philosophy and work ethic. But personal change is much harder to achieve. Sadly, it's not something that's done with signs, protests, and pieces on the evening news. Personal change is achieved through frank but respectful dinner table conversations and tavern dialogue. Individuals are walled off, largely for good reason, when they're not in the company of their loved ones. Letting your guard down around the wrong stranger can lead to dire physical and emotional consequences. But many of us come home at the end of the day and let our hair down around our spouses, immediate family members, and close friends. This is an incredible luxury, especially in the modern world.

Now that politics seems to be at the forefront of all conversation these days, we need to find a way to work certain viewpoints into our more vulnerable discussions. This doesn't need to, and quite frankly can't, be formal or forced. The walls go right back up when someone feels that they're being sold something. But most of our loved ones have enough respect for us to have deep discussions of life and philosophy. In fact, this is where a great deal of our moral foundation and growth as human beings come from. Political change can be achieved in this forum, as well, and it may be the only way to disinfect some of the more nefarious political beliefs that have infested our loved ones' brains.

The key to achieve this goal is mutual respect. If you come out of your corner swinging, the other person is either going to dig their heels in and stay with their current position or just tap out of the conversation entirely. Instead, if you come to the discussion with an open mind and make it clear that you want to honestly exchange ideas and perspectives, you're far more likely to have a positive outcome. Think of a person's actual beliefs and outlooks as a crown jewel hidden behind layers and layers of security. Those layers are made up of social expectations, fear, and uncertainty among many other things. But if you can get someone in the right frame of mind and actually have a productive discussion, you may just be able to change their mind.

There's something very important to remember here, though. You will not change a person's perspective in one conversation. You likely won't even change it in several conversations. The goal is to have enough conversations that your loved one sees the light of reason gradually over time. That's the only way this stuff sticks. We've all seen TV shows where people talk about a complicated topic and reach a consensus in half an hour, including commercials. That just doesn't happen in the real world. The stakes are higher here and, quite frankly, you have to have a lot of respect for a person if you're going to go to the lengths necessary to get them to understand why their beliefs are based in flawed logic.

Odds are your family member is not directly responsible for the evils that Republicans have foisted on all of us. Unless you are personally related to a Republican politician, your loved one likely is just a supporter, knowing or unknowing, of the despicable policies and political structures detailed earlier in this book. As a result, it's important to remember that you are, in fact, discussing these issues with a loved one and not a hateful stranger on the street. But it is equally important to remember that your family member is part of the problem. They likely don't view themselves that way. Nonetheless, Republican evil depends on the masses that give support to their heinous agenda in countless ways. People of color, women, and poor people are suffering due to the ideologies that your loved ones likely support. It is possible to compartmentalize the love you have for your families with the hatred you have for the results of their political beliefs. After all, isn't it religious Republicans who so often say "hate the sin, love the sinner"?

I'll end by saying this: If you're going to undertake to try to change your loved one's minds, please do so carefully. You have to use a combination of assertive dialogue and appropriate tact. You can't risk coming off as soft, but you can't approach the topic with so much fervor that you alienate the person you're talking to. This balance is important because tipping the scales too far in either direction risks bungling the whole pursuit. As someone who is not a rich, white man, I and a bunch of other people like me are depending on you to get this right. Obviously, you're not required to do anything. You can continue to let your loved ones do and believe terrible things. But if you really want to dedicate yourself to ending these behavior patterns in those you love the most, please tread carefully. You shouldn't have to be in this position, but we are all depending on you.

ABOUT THE AUTHOR

Juniper Lewis is an author and political commentator dedicated to fighting back against repression and oppression in all forms. He was galvanized by the election of Donald Trump to resist the negative policies that threatened him and so many people he cares about. Juniper recognizes his privilege, but vows to check it at the door. This is his first of many books. Be on the lookout for more.

 twitter.com/realjuniperlewis